Getting into University

Art & Design Courses

Clare McEwan

14th edition

Getting into University: Art & Design Courses

This 14th edition published in 2026 by Trotman, an imprint of Trotman Indigo Publishing Ltd, 18e Charles Street, Bath, BA1 1HX

© Trotman Indigo Publishing Ltd 2026

Authors: Clare McEwan
12th–13th edns: Greg Ioannou and James Foster
11th edn: Mark Cheeseman and Louise de la Hey
4th–10th edns: James Burnett
3rd edn: James Burnett and Jonathan Hollins
1st–2nd edns: Jonathan Hollins

British Library Cataloguing in Publication Data
A catalogue record for this book is available from the British Library

Paperback ISBN 978 1 911724 93 3
eISBN 978 1 911724 94 0

All rights reserved. This book is sold subject to the condition that it shall not, by way of trade or otherwise, be lent, resold, hired out or otherwise circulated without the publisher's prior written consent in any form of binding or cover other than that in which it is published and without a similar condition including this condition being imposed on the subsequent purchaser. No part of this publication may be reproduced, stored in a retrieval system or transmitted in any form or by any means, electronic and mechanical, photocopying, recording or otherwise without prior permission of Trotman Indigo Publishing.

Every effort has been made to trace copyright holders and to obtain their permission for the use of copyright material. The publisher apologises for any errors or omissions and would be grateful to be notified of any corrections that should be incorporated in future editions of this book.

The authorised representative in the EEA is Easy Access System Europe Oü (EAS), Mustamäe tee 50, 10621 Tallinn, Estonia.

Printed and bound in the UK by 4edge Ltd, Hockley, Essex

All details in this book were correct at the time of going to press. To keep up to date with all the latest news and updates and to access the online resources that accompany this book, use this QR code or visit **www.trotman.co.uk/pages/getting-into-online-resources**.

Contents

About the author	vi
Acknowledgements	vii
Introduction	**1**
What is this book about?	2
Routes for art and design students	2
Who is this book for?	3
How should I use this book?	3
1| Careers in art and design	**4**
Considering your career options	5
What do art and design graduates do?	6
Where might your degree lead?	6
'Working as an artist...'	8
'Working as a designer ...'	10
Further research	11
Guidance on applying for work experience	15
2| Foundation courses	**16**
What can you expect from a Foundation course and why do you need one?	16
Choosing a Foundation course	21
Making the final selection	24
Entry requirements	26
Checklist	26
3| Degree courses	**27**
Where are you now?	27
What is a degree course?	27
What can you expect from a degree course?	29
Entry requirements	29
Degree course specialisations	30
Foundation degrees	31
Degree apprenticeships	32
Finding the right course	33
The final choice	36
Checklist	38
4| Architecture	**39**
Qualifying as an architect	39
Entry requirements	41
Preparation for your application	42

	Alternative architecture courses	42
	The personal statement	43
	Graduate employment	49
5|	**How to apply**	**50**
	Foundation courses	50
	Degree and HND courses	51
	The personal statement	51
	Scottish art schools and colleges	59
	Non-standard applications	59
	Preparation for your application	60
6|	**International students**	**61**
	Application deadlines	62
	Portfolio submissions and interviews	62
	Alternative routes	63
	English language requirements	64
	Visas	64
7|	**Putting together a portfolio**	**66**
	What is a portfolio?	66
	Which portfolio should you buy?	67
	Getting your work together	67
	Matching your portfolio to the course specification	70
	Enrolling on short courses	73
	Portfolio reviews	73
	Freak-outs	74
	Foundation course portfolios	76
	Specialist course portfolios	77
	Checklist	82
8|	**The interview**	**83**
	What is the purpose of the interview?	83
	What to expect	84
	Preparing	84
	The interview itself – some tips	87
	Checklist	90
9|	**Offers and what to do on results day**	**91**
	When the results are available	91
	Foundation courses	91
	Degree courses	93
10|	**Fees and funding**	**98**
	UK (home) students	98
	Living expenses	99
	Funding your studies	100
	Postgraduate courses	102
	The Turing Scheme	103
	Other sources of funding	103

11|	**Postgraduate courses**	**104**
	Types of course	104
	Applying for a postgraduate course	105
12|	**Further information**	**108**
	Applications	108
	Funding	109
	International students	109
	Art and design bodies	109
	Architecture	111
	Reading list	111
	Magazines	112
	Websites	112
	Artists' websites	113
	Appendix 1: Institution contact details	**114**
	Appendix 2: Glossary	**128**
	Studying art and design	128
	Ways of describing art and design	129

About the author

Clare McEwan graduated with a BA in Graphic Design and Illustration in 2000 and began her career as a freelance illustrator. In 2003, she completed a Postgraduate Certificate in Education (Art and Design, Secondary) at the University of Central England, Birmingham, and has since built a successful career in teaching.

Over the past two decades, Clare has taught A Level Fine Art, Graphic Communication and Photography, as well as GCSE Fine Art and Photography. She has extensive experience supporting both UK and international students through the application process for art Foundation and creative degree courses, offering guidance on portfolio development, preparing for interviews and making the most of open days.

In 2008, Clare earned an MA in Graphic Communication from Nottingham Trent University. She is currently Head of Art at MPW Cambridge and continues to develop her own artistic practice alongside her teaching career.

Acknowledgements

This book would not have been possible without the involvement of a great many people. In particular, I would like to thank James Burnett, the original author and factual compiler of the information, much of which continues to be relevant in this edition. Jonathan Hollins, who was a principal contributor to and the driving force behind the first edition of this book, and Beryl Dixon for her work on the second edition and the earlier incarnation of the book. Thank you also to Is Bealey, Annette Bellwood, Debbie Cook, Robert Green, Sarah Horton, Astrid MacKellar, Andrew Watson and Natalie Wyle for their expertise, help, advice and written contributions. Our colleagues in MPW's art department provided contributions to the book and helpful advice on preparing students for their art school applications. A particular mention to Greg Ioannou, who has generously given so much help and time to support his colleagues at MPW and has also had a huge impact on this book. Thank you also to Seb Antoniou, Steve O' Connor, Geraint Evans, James Foster, Fergus Hare, Anna Lytridou, Michael Milloy, Alex Mullins and Johanna Parv for their contributions on the rewards and demands of working as artists and designers. Finally, thank you to all the wonderful students who kindly shared their experiences, including Dariga A, Nikan A, Lottie C, Nazar E, Adam G, Honor H, Abdullah K, Annabel K, Saroushka L, Lucy M, Anna R, Holly R, Haya S, Jess Z and, most recently, Grace C, Alina K, Kabriella L and Vanessa Y. Having the opportunity to work with such brilliant students makes teaching art a truly wonderful profession.

Clare McEwan, March 2026

Introduction

Art and design are constantly evolving, shaped by the rapid pace of technology. Yet even the most advanced innovations depend on the creativity of artists and designers to bring ideas to life. The exciting reality is that you may soon play a vital role in that process. Your journey begins here.

New technologies are revealing fresh ways for people to connect, communicate and express themselves. Artists and designers are central to this: not only do they shape the visual identity of these platforms, but they also question how such innovations affect us, how they can be used and what they reveal about being human. By sparking dialogue, exploring possibilities and reimagining our relationship with technology, artists and designers help define the cultural landscape of the future.

This relationship between creativity and innovation is nothing new. From the earliest illuminated manuscripts to carved hieroglyphs, visual guidance has always been essential. Today, our homes, workplaces and journeys are filled with objects and technologies that have been carefully designed: the chair you sit on, the desk or table you lean on, even the computer you use. Functionality is everywhere, but it is design and aesthetic choice that makes our environment meaningful, personal and inspiring.

Graduates of art and design go on to careers as varied as fashion marketing, art restoration, web design, advertising and architecture. Others take their first steps into independent practice, creating and selling their own work through small design studios or craft businesses.

Furthering your education on a creative pathway is the beginning of a journey of invention, discovery and self-expression. You may already be drawn to a particular discipline, whether fine art, film, fashion or textiles. Or perhaps you are still exploring, driven by a need to experiment with colour, line, form, pattern and shape. Wherever you are on this path, this book is designed to guide and inspire you.

What is this book about?

You may be asking yourself the following questions.

- Which course(s) should I take?
- Where should I apply to study?
- What should I include in my portfolio?
- How do I prepare for an interview?

This book offers practical answers to these questions and many others and aims to guide you successfully through the application process.

Routes for art and design students

Entry to an art and design degree is usually a little more complicated than entry to other degree courses – that is one of the reasons why this book has been written. Figure 1 gives an overview of the range of entry routes available; each of these will be examined in detail as the book progresses.

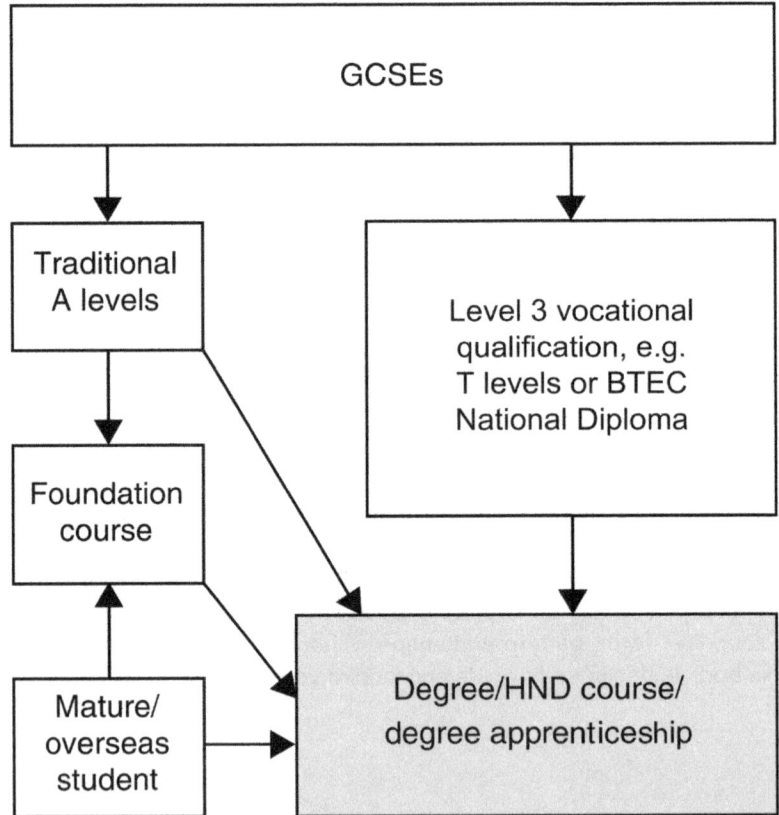

Figure 1 Entry routes

Who is this book for?

This book covers the procedure for applications for both foundation studies and undergraduate degree courses in art and design, and for students thinking about architecture. If you are currently studying at A level, you will find all chapters of this guide relevant. If you are studying for the BTEC National Diploma or a similar qualification, you may be tempted not to read Chapter 2. However, it is recommended that you do read it, because it will help you to know what other students have been up to. The entry routes for architecture courses are outlined in Chapter 4.

If you are a student applying from outside the UK or a mature student, you will have to think about some other considerations. Most of what is contained in this book will apply, and there is additional information in Chapter 6 and the 'Non-standard applications' section in Chapter 5. Throughout the book, the entrance procedures have been illustrated with reference to A levels, but the information is equally relevant to students studying for Scottish Highers, the International Baccalaureate or the Irish Leaving Certificate. If you have any questions about whether your academic qualifications will satisfy the art schools, you should contact them directly.

How should I use this book?

Read it. No, really! Just having the book on the shelf will not get you into art school. Discuss the information and ideas contained within it. Speak to your tutors, friends and parents. You will find it helpful to talk things through. Certain chapters have checklists: use these to help you keep track of your progress. Above all, take action – and when you have finished the book, you should have a clear idea of where action is needed. If, for example, you realise that you probably need to do some more life drawing, then go and do some. Admissions tutors are, in any case, always interested in the work applicants have done in their own time, that is, not just pieces they have done for A level coursework or exams.

You will feel far more confident about your application if you know that you have done everything that you possibly can to help yourself, and reading this book – then acting on what you find out – is the best way to start.

1 | Careers in art and design

Wherever you are right now, take a look around you. Look closely at the environment you are in and think about the contribution made to your surroundings by artists and designers. Some may be obvious: there might be a painting on the wall or the light fitting hanging from your ceiling. Look at the clothes you're wearing. Who was responsible for the cut and style? Who designed the fastening on your trousers? Where would you be without that? At home, consider the ergonomic design of your laptop and the artwork for the music that you download on it. Think about the packaging of the food that you eat and the shape of the cutlery that you eat with. Who took the fashion photographs in the magazine that you have just read? Who created the cover design? Who designed the logo? You may have done some research on art schools before reading this chapter – those websites were all designed by someone.

Artists and designers do not just exhibit their work in galleries and exhibitions. They are involved in almost all aspects of our day-to-day living. Artists and designers are concerned with how things look, feel and function. Virtually everything that is manufactured is designed to some extent. Most elements of the media – newspapers, magazines, television, websites, advertising – have considerable input from artists and designers. For every household name that emerges from art school to become rich and famous, there are many thousands of graduates who take up exciting careers that allow them to use their creative talents.

Studying a creative subject will also give you skills and approaches that are valuable in many careers that are not directly 'creative'. You will learn how to communicate using visual information, and you will gain analytical and problem-solving skills. Importantly, by studying alongside other creative people, you will learn to trust your own ideas and to work independently.

If you plan to study something like mathematics at university (but, as you are reading this book, you probably don't!), you don't need to have a definite idea of what you want to do after graduating, because a mathematics degree can lead to hundreds of different careers other than banking, finance or management, including those that are not directly related to the subject. But a degree in costume for performance, for example, offers you fewer options, so you need to be reasonably sure that a career as a ballet or theatre costume designer is what you are aiming for. Gaining work experience prior to your application is, therefore, not only important in convincing the selectors that you are serious but also will ensure you are heading in a direction that is right for you. If you are passionate about research into make-up, for example, and know that this is the only thing you want to do, then choose the degree course in cosmetic science, rather than something less focused.

Most universities offer excellent careers advice (for example, have a look at the resources section for graduates on the University of the Arts London website: www.arts.ac.uk/student-jobs-and-careers), but in the case of art and design students, it is important to have thought about possible careers before choosing a degree course. This is why the Foundation course is an important aspect of an art education, because it gives you time to look at degree courses in more detail before committing yourself. Many art and design degree courses are very specialised and will give you a relatively narrow range of options, so you need to be sure that you are choosing a degree course that is going to get you where you want to be.

Considering your career options

A helpful approach when considering career options is to appreciate that the creative skills you possess are key skills. Your ability to understand and communicate using visual language is as fundamental as being able to understand and use mathematics.

Your talents will always be needed, especially when people are exploring new ideas. Landing on the moon, for example, was a great technological achievement and may not at first seem to have much to do with art and design – but you can be sure that designers were involved every step of the way. Think about it – a footwear designer would have helped to design Neil Armstrong's space boots; perhaps they went on to work for Gucci! Looking at things in this way will help you keep an open mind.

Most students who apply to art and design courses do so because they have a passion for art and the ability to be creative. Some students say that their intention, after graduating, is to 'become an artist', by which they mean that they would like to use their creative skills in a way that is not manipulated by financial or corporate issues – perhaps they intend to have their own studio, to exhibit their work and to become respected and admired by those who understand and value what they create. Realistically, however, not everyone has the talent, the focus, the energy or the luck to make a living in this way, but this is only one of the options available to those completing a course in art and design.

What do art and design graduates do?

A reasonably high proportion of art and design graduates work on a freelance basis or are self-employed (see the section 'Working as an artist …' on page 8). This can be extremely stimulating and satisfying because you can, to a certain extent, pick and choose the type of work that you wish to undertake. However, it can also be stressful at times because you will need to combine your creative expertise with your skills in business. For some, this is not always a good combination.

Generally, employment rates for art and design graduates are pretty good; most will be able to find work shortly after graduating – although you need to bear in mind that for some, this will mean involvement in short-term projects or contracts.

The Higher Education Statistics Agency (HESA) publishes an annual graduate outcomes survey – What do graduates do? – which collects data on graduate activity 15 months after their graduation. Data from graduates of the 2022/23 academic year who studied in the Creative Arts and Design field show that, of those who responded to the survey, 43% were in full-time employment, 28% were in part-time employment, 3% pursued full-time further study and 9% combined employment and study. Only 7% were unemployed (www.hesa.ac.uk/news/17-07-2025/sb272-higher-education-graduate-outcomes-statistics/study). Further information can be found at www.prospects.ac.uk/careers-advice/what-can-i-do-with-my-degree.

Other art and design graduates were working in a variety of jobs, including marketing, sales, public relations, commercial and public-sector management, buying, retailing, catering and general administrative work. In other words, some were using their degrees as a generalist qualification and others were in temporary employment – just like graduates in other subjects. A list of publications that provide information on careers and employment rates is given in Chapter 12.

Where might your degree lead?

For the purpose of career options, degree courses can be divided into two categories: the fine arts and the applied arts. Examples of the first category include painting, drawing and sculpture, and some photography and textile courses. The second category includes an enormous range of options such as communications, fashion design, furniture design, art restoration, jewellery design, television and film design, photojournalism and architectural photography. On many of these applied courses, you will be developing skills specifically designed to help you meet employers' needs. If your degree falls into the second category, then you may well find businesses that are looking for someone with your specific qualifications. However, as a fine art

1| Careers in Art and Design

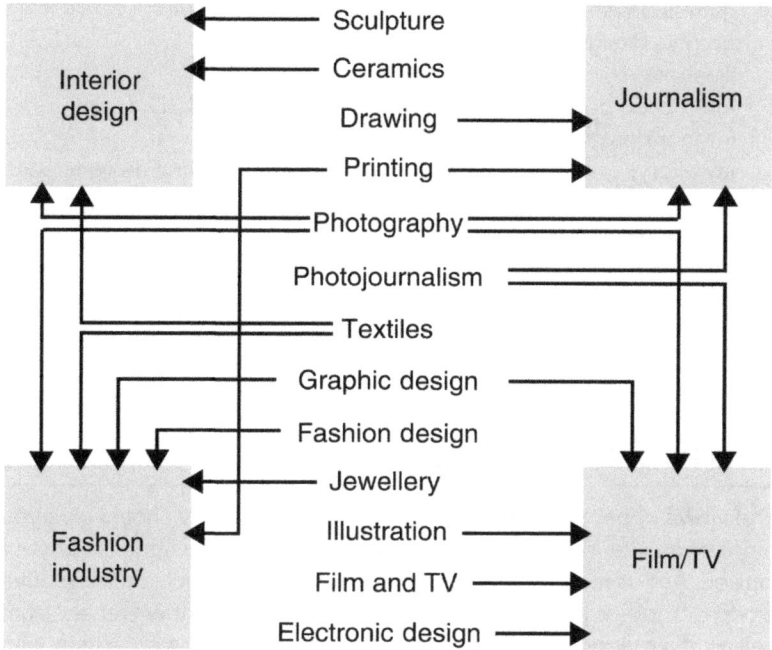

Figure 2 Job opportunities

student who, say, used digital manipulation techniques extensively in your work, you can apply to companies that are as interested in your thorough understanding of that particular software program as they are in your overall digital manipulation skills. This 'cross-over' ability demonstrates the value of key skills and will greatly increase your chances of having a successful working life.

The creative and visual communication skills that art and design graduates possess also make them very suitable for a range of interesting jobs within the field of art and design, such as:

- museum or gallery curator;
- museum or gallery guide;
- art director for magazines, TV or film;
- researcher for TV arts programmes;
- arts journalist or reviewer;
- arts events organiser.

Figure 2 will give you some idea of the range of job sectors to which specific degree courses might lead you.

Some of the careers that you might consider are:

- animation;
- architecture;
- branding;
- costume design;
- curation;
- exhibition design;
- fashion design;
- games design;

- games development;
- graphic design;
- illustration;
- interaction design;
- interior design;
- jewellery;
- journalism;
- model-making;
- newspaper and magazine design;
- photography;
- printmaking;
- product design;
- public arts;
- publishing;
- sculpture and 3D design;
- teaching;
- textile and fabric design;
- theatre and performance design;
- user experience design;
- video and film production;
- visual effects;
- web design.

'Working as an artist...'

The views of people working as artists included below should give you more of an idea of what to expect and how to make a success of your career. And remember, many artists need to combine their creative work with other jobs because they cannot support themselves from selling their work. Others choose to combine careers as artists with work in other fields because it helps them to gain a sense of perspective in their creative processes.

> 'There is no one model for an artist's career. Artists face many challenges, but they continue to survive and thrive, and they do this through a range of means. Artists' careers are often cyclical – for most artists, a career has its ups and downs and takes many forms.
>
> 'It all starts in the studio with some fundamental questions that you address through your practical artwork and critical thinking: What kind of work do you make? What are your key subjects/ideas/research? What are your contexts and who are your peers? How do you disseminate your work? Who is your audience? How do you create an effective professional network? Art college can give you the time, space and support to begin to answer these questions.
>
> 'Artists often do a range of things within their practices: making artworks, exhibiting, writing, curation, working in academia, presenting papers, giving talks and so on. Artists can also have opportunities to work with other media outside their core practice or to engage in collaborative or cross-disciplinary projects.
>
> 'Additionally, artists are often also engaged in a range of jobs across the art world and creative industries, both as a way of supporting their practice but also as their predominant career choice: arts administration, artist support, museum and gallery work, art production, writing, teaching, academic research, curation and so on. It can be very rewarding to have different projects on the

go, but establishing a productive balance between your various commitments is a perennial challenge.

'You can't wait for opportunities to fall into your lap, you have to make multiple applications for opportunities posted in listings sites such as Artquest, a-n, Arts Jobs and Arts News, Re-title. You can also initiate your own projects; for example, organising group exhibitions can be a productive first step for early career artists. Many well-known projects and organisations (for example galleries, residencies, studios and workshops) have been initiated by proactive artists to fill gaps and create opportunities and resources where none had existed before.

'It is important to familiarise yourself with the current debates and trends in the art world by looking at art-related websites, podcasts, magazines and journals, and by attending private views and visiting as many galleries and events as possible.

'Networks of fellow artists and arts professionals are very useful for supporting your career and can be initially established at college with your peers, and then through group shows, studio groups, critical forums, conferences, residencies or through the social side of the art world. Art can be a truly nurturing and fulfilling career that can introduce you to a wide range of engaging people and take you to fascinating places. But you do need a degree of resilience, fortitude and resourcefulness.'

Geraint Evans, Artist and Pathway Leader for MA
Fine Art Painting at Camberwell College of Arts

'I couldn't wait to get to art school and to finally be surrounded by people like me and be given the opportunity to learn about and make art every day.

'However, I think the most important time for me was the year or two straight after I had left. Enjoy art school, and get everything out of it that you can, and as soon as you leave, get a space for you to work in and find a way to be in there every day continuing your practice. Make the art that you want to make. Don't concern yourself too much with what other artists are doing. Today we are bombarded with images via our phones, and it's too much, and it's distracting and unnecessary. Don't compare your art and achievements with other people's. You don't have their skills and thoughts, and they don't have yours. Everyone's career is different.

'Let your work evolve. Life changes all the time and there's no reason why you can't be expected to either.'

Fergus Hare, Painter

'Since graduating with a Fine Art degree back in 2001, I've worked as a painter, teacher, animator (among other things!) and I've now established myself as a freelance commercial illustrator and storyboard artist. I love the diversity of my clients and projects (including Amazon, Bentley and Coca Cola). This ranges from drawing TV adverts to producing logos, medical illustrations and designs for fashion brands! I'm also creatively fulfilled within my work, which is a huge plus.

'I think there are currently so many opportunities in the art and design industries and it's the perfect time to explore what's out there and leave your stamp on the world. It can be difficult and frustrating at times (like all jobs!) but I really appreciate the freedom and variety that my career brings. Being freelance can bring more uncertainty than being employed, so you should consider if that's a good fit for you.

'Going to university to study a creative course, doing an apprenticeship or working for a creative company will give you so many transferable skills for your career. It's not just about improving your technical skills – learning how to collaborate, being professional and organised and having any other experiences will be incredibly useful for your creative journey. Absorb everything you can from your peers, tutors and employers and this will help shape you into a successful artist. Go for it.'

Seb Antoniou, storyboard artist and
commercial illustrator

'Working as a designer ...'

The views of people working as designers provided below should give you more of an idea of what to expect in the world of design, and how to make a success of your career.

Steve O'Connor is a Senior UX Design Consultant at Version 1. He began at art college studying graphic design and illustration before an unexpected detour into retail management – a crash course in understanding people! After teaching product designers 3D software, he returned to graphic and web design and eventually found his way into user experience design. Today, he designs accessible, inclusive digital products and services that put people first. His clients have included Conran Design, the BBC, Mind, AstraZeneca and the Department for Education.

'A career in design isn't always a straight path. Exploring other avenues along the way can make you a far stronger designer.

'Design itself isn't straightforward either. More a loop-the-loop of ideas, feedback and the occasional bit of panic! The key is to stay curious. Find what interests you, keep asking lots of questions, practice active listening and accept that you'll never know it all. There are always new methods, new problems and new tools.

'You learn to let go of ego fairly quickly. What matters isn't what you like personally, but what's right for the user or the client – and you will be wrong sometimes. Accept it. Collaboration is where the magic happens. You'll get further by building on others' ideas, or letting them build on yours, than by protecting your own.

'Always be creative, but always be practical. Sometimes you'll have the freedom to go wild (enjoy it!) and other times you'll be working within tight constraints. Both can be just as satisfying if you approach them with an open mind and a genuine desire to make something great.'

Steve O'Connor, Senior UX Design Consultant

Alex Mullins reimagines and handcrafts handsome clothing. Educated at Central Saint Martins and the Royal College of Art, he set up his eponymous brand in 2014. Mullins' clothes take inspiration from real life, editing the everyday to rework the classic wardrobe.

Alex develops textiles through innovative methods that resonate with the feeling of the 'handmade'. He playfully builds concepts around his clothes, with a heavy focus on cut, colour and distortion.

'If I could give any advice to young people wanting a career in design it would be "NEVER GIVE UP". You will always have setbacks and disappointments but, as with anything in life, if you want something you have to work for it and not be disappointed if things don't go your way – just learn from it.

'Design is a challenging industry, and what I have seen from others in the business in recent times is a brilliant change in attitude. Support each other, be professional and have respect for those around you. When you're good at what you do and have faith in that then there is no need not to work together. Building contacts and connections will give you a well-needed helping hand at many stages of your career, and nurturing these relationships is important.

'Most importantly, HAVE FUN, and don't lose your vision.'

Alex Mullins, fashion designer

Further research

If you are sure that you want a career in a creative field, but unsure about the exact field at the point when you're trying to choose your degree course, then it might be better to choose something more general, such as fine art or graphic design. In order to get a better idea about possible careers, your research could include:

- doing work experience;
- talking to school or college careers departments;
- looking at university websites;
- talking to practitioners;
- visiting professional bodies (such as the Design Council – see Chapter 12 for contact details);
- taking a one-year art Foundation course (see Chapter 2).

Work experience and internships

If you are considering a career in art or design, you should take every opportunity available to gain work experience, internships or other relevant experience. There are two reasons for this.

1. You will find it easier to convince potential employers and university admissions staff that you are serious about a career or study in your chosen field if you can demonstrate that you have investigated it thoroughly.
2. You will have the chance to see whether the path that you have chosen is right for you.

Getting work experience or internships will require you to do a lot of investigation and to use your contacts, parents' contacts and teachers to help you. Being shy or passive and hoping that opportunities will knock on your door is unlikely to work. Having the courage to demonstrate your talent and creativity to people you do not know is something you will need if you want to have a career as an artist or designer, so, as well as being an important part of your journey into art and design, it is also a vital quality for a successful career.

What should you look for?

- Part-time work in galleries, at exhibitions or art shows.
- Part-time work in other creative environments, such as advertising agencies, architecture firms, magazine publishers, fashion companies and interior design businesses.
- Opportunities to help set up school or college art shows.
- Work on blogs, websites or other social media.

'After graduating from MPW, I received offers from all the universities I applied to and chose to continue my studies at Central Saint Martins, where I am pursuing a BA in Jewellery Design. Having completed my first and second years, I am currently undertaking my placement year at Yoko London, an internationally

1| Careers in Art and Design

recognised pearl jewellery brand celebrated for its craftsmanship and contemporary design.

'My experience at Central Saint Martins has been profoundly transformative. The course has challenged me to view jewellery not merely as an adornment, but as a form of creative expression – a medium through which stories, identities and cultural values can be communicated. The programme encourages independence of thought, material exploration and concept-driven design – qualities first nurtured during my time at MPW.

'At MPW, I felt supported both personally and academically. My art tutors fostered creative freedom while offering structured and individualised guidance. I was encouraged to experiment, take risks and refine my artistic voice. That balance of encouragement and discipline, combined with the technical and critical-thinking skills I developed there, established a strong foundation for my progression into higher education and the professional world.

'Currently, during my placement year at Yoko London, I have gained invaluable insight into the workings of the fine jewellery industry. I have been involved in aspects of design development and production, learning first-hand the importance of craftsmanship, precision and collaboration within a luxury design context. This experience has allowed me to connect my academic learning with real-world practice and to deepen my understanding of how creative ideas evolve into finished collections.

'I would encourage current students to seek opportunities that extend beyond their formal studies – whether through internships, placements or creative collaborations. Engaging with the industry early provides not only practical experience but also a broader perspective on potential career paths within the arts. Taking initiative to gain exposure in professional settings builds confidence, develops essential skills and helps to identify where one's true interests and strengths lie.'

Kabriella L, BA Jewellery Design, Central St Martins

'I am currently in my final year studying Games Art and Design at Norwich University of the Arts (NUA). Apart from honing one's creative and technical abilities, university is also a great place to make connections with industry professionals.

'I had the opportunity to complete a one-month internship at Odd Bug Studio as an Art Renderer. Throughout the internship, I attended weekly meetings where I received constructive feedback from professionals on how to improve my work and bring it up to industry standards. It was truly a valuable experience that allowed me to push my technical abilities further.

'I am currently building my portfolio to showcase my work in 3D environmental art, as my goal is to become an environment artist at a major game studio one day. Whenever you get the chance, talk to professionals and show them your portfolio – even if you think it's not good enough. It's always good to let them remember you, as it might open up more opportunities in the future!'

Vanessa Y, BA Games Art and Design,
Norwich University

Advice when choosing internships

- 'Aim for at least three months so that you have enough time to get to know a company.
- Try and find somewhere that pays travel expenses / lunch expenses, as you will not be paid a salary.
- Really research the company you want to intern for and find blogs where previous interns talk about what they did there and what they learnt. I know many people who saved up money to intern in London and then ended up making coffee for three months and learnt nothing.
- Speak with your tutors about the best places to intern as they may have a contact there or may have sent students there in the past and can let you know what to expect – my tutor's advice was not to apply to certain companies due to previous bad experiences of past students.
- When interning, if you're not gaining experience in the area you want to be in, speak up – for example, if they put you to assist the pattern cutter but you want to be assisting the print designer – which is actually really nerve-racking, but important.
- If you work for a small company, you will gain experience in all areas and get a much more hands-on approach, but if you work for a larger company, you may get to do less but you may have a better chance of getting a job with them after you graduate.
- Be as niche as possible – if you want to get into menswear and love digital print, find a company that specialises in digitally printed men's shirts.'

Annabel K, BA Fashion

1| Careers in Art and Design

Guidance on applying for work experience

What should you include in your email and covering letter? In the first instance, address your email to someone specific rather than a general title. Attach your covering letter and CV, as emails should be kept concise. For example:

> Dear Ms Smith
>
> I am a student studying A levels in Art, French and Geography at St Benedict's School, and am looking for summer holiday work experience in the field of art and design.
>
> For further information, please refer to covering letter and CV (attached).
>
> I would be most grateful if you could let me know at your earliest convenience if your organisation can offer any work experience.
>
> Regards,
> Jamelia James

In your covering letter you should include a short profile (approximately six lines) in which you should sound confident and demonstrate your motivation, commitment and enthusiasm. Remember to mention any IT skills relevant to your application, for example, Photoshop, Lightroom, camera use and so on. You could also mention an example where you exhibited problem-solving skills – this is applicable to all forms of work experience. State that you are willing to help out whatever the task, and talk about how you enjoy working as part of a team.

Feel free to mention any social media (Instagram, Facebook, etc.) you engage with. Do mention if you have edited or created a web design, a blog, a vlog and so on. Make sure that if you give out your social media links, there is nothing on there that would make you regret doing so.

2 | Foundation courses

Art and design Foundation courses – the full name being Level 3 Diploma in Foundation Studies (Art and Design) – provide a bridge between the kind of study undertaken at GCSE and A level and the type of work you will do on courses offered at degree level. Although there are exceptions, for those of you currently studying general A levels and hoping to get into art school, taking up a place on a Foundation course will be your next step. Most typically, they are self-contained one-year courses available at a variety of different types of institutions, including universities, art schools and colleges of further and higher education.

What can you expect from a Foundation course and why do you need one?

You can expect to have a lot of fun on the Foundation course. While each course will have its own individual style, all Foundation courses will attempt to challenge and develop your critical awareness and creative skills. A Foundation course will give you an opportunity to discover much more about your creative interests and abilities by giving you the chance to experiment with different fields of the creative arts, as well as explore methods and materials that will not have been previously available to you. You will have the freedom to explore your own ideas and will be truly working for yourself.

There is probably no better way to prepare for a specialist degree course than by completing Foundation studies. The course will develop your abilities and give you more of an understanding of your own direction; it will help you select a specialist area of study, prepare your portfolio and make applications for degree courses. Take a look at the views of these students.

> 'At first, I didn't know what a Foundation course was, I always knew I wanted to study fashion design, but I wasn't sure whether I should opt for textile design or womenswear. Having a year full of experimentation and self-discovery helped me realise my strengths and interests. Coming from Estonia, it was a new experience for me to live in London and it was very intense and exciting. We did a lot of short projects, with deadlines every two weeks. The course taught me self-discipline, and I learnt to organise my thoughts and ideas as

a designer. One of the most important skills I acquired was keeping a daily notebook and sketchbook, documenting all my thoughts and ideas. My tutors helped me along the way and always knew how to push me in the right direction so that I felt more inspired and creative.

'The Foundation year was a good opportunity to meet new people from all over the world. And for many, it was the first time away from home. A lot of my current friends and colleagues are people I met on the Foundation course.'

Johanna P, Central Saint Martins Foundation

'I really wanted to study BA Fashion Womenswear at Central Saint Martins (CSM) after studying art, textiles and photography at A level. In order to apply to the BA course, it is compulsory to undertake a Foundation course, which is a great way to get a really good feel for what the BA course might look like. On the Foundation course at CSM, we are being taught how to generate concepts and really look at where our inspiration comes from and how you can harness these inspirations and expand on them. We are looking closely at form of pattern and shapes and different and new ways of structuring, with more than just fashion in mind – it has everything to do with the outside world and what you want your place to be in it. At CSM there's a deliberate absence of rigid rules; instead, a culture is cultivated that encourages thinking beyond conventional boundaries. This Foundation programme is instructing us on the art of conceptualisation and probing the origins of our inspiration.

'Being at CSM has already brought opportunities to design for real life in hugely exciting ways while being around some very talented individuals who are inspiring and encourage you to constantly bring your best and original work to the table each day. It is giving me an amazing insight into what life at CSM and beyond could look like.'

Lottie C, Art (Fashion) Foundation student,
Central St Martins

'The Central St Martins Foundation Course at UAL stands as an unparalleled opportunity for students navigating their academic journey. When I initially applied, my sights were set on architecture, yet an unforeseen rejection from my preferred university left me re-evaluating my path. Opting for the Foundation course at UAL proved transformative. Rather than narrowing my focus, I embraced a diagnostic approach. Over the first six weeks, I immersed myself in diverse pathways encompassing fine art, fashion, textiles and architecture. This immersive experience allowed me to make an informed decision about my future career direction. Week by week, engaging with professors across disciplines and scrutinising *previous students' works illuminated potential paths. It was during the eighth week that I discovered my passion lay in jewellery, footwear and fashion accessories.*

'My journey at UAL wasn't just about revelation; it was also about the resources and support that fostered growth. The institution provided an array of facilities – metal, wood and plastic workshops – coupled with experienced technicians who helped translate ideas into tangible creations, mirroring the standards envisioned in my designs. Moreover, comprehensive student support services were instrumental in navigating challenges. Collaborating with the academic support team was pivotal in refining my research skills, understanding the importance of thorough research and accessing the vast library resources efficiently.'

Haya S, Graduate, Central St
Martins Art Foundation

How Foundation courses are organised

Colleges vary in the ways in which they organise their courses, but in nearly all cases, you will choose from the following areas of study:

- **Art**: painting, sculpture and drawing; possibly also film and photography.
- **Communication**: graphic design, illustration and film and photography media.
- **Design**: fashion, product design, ceramics and jewellery.

Course content is standardised to a certain extent, in accordance with the regulations of the four awarding bodies that validate courses in England, Wales and Northern Ireland. These are Pearson, the Welsh Joint Education Committee (WJEC), the University of the Arts London (UAL) and Ascentis*. Under their regulations, Foundation courses are divided into three phases, each phase being roughly equivalent to one of the three terms that make up the academic year. (See Table 1.)

The exploratory phase will give you a general introduction to the theory and practice of art and design. You will have the chance to experiment with a wide range of materials you may not have had the opportunity to use before – including plaster, wood, metal and ceramics, for example – and will work on projects designed to help you identify your strengths and interests. In the second or pathway phase, you will investigate a specialist area of art and design practice, guided by a tutor experienced in that field. At this stage of the course, you will also begin to put together a portfolio for degree course applications.

Last comes the confirmatory phase, during which you will complete your portfolio, work on a major project (usually negotiated with your specialist tutor) and put together an end-of-year show. The build-up to the end-of-year show and the show itself are things that you won't

Table 1 Summary of Foundation course structure

Provider	First Stage	Second Stage	Third Stage
Pearson (8 units with some optional units)	Unit 1: Visual Recording and Communication Unit 2: Critical and Contextual Studies in Art and Design	Unit 3: The Creative Process Unit 4: Materials, Techniques and Process in Art and Design	Optional Units: Learners must complete two optional units from a choice of eight subject pathways
WJEC (6 units)	Unit 1: Drawing and Colour as an Investigative Process Unit 2: Exploring Materials and Making	Unit 3: Developing Specialist Practice and Preparing for Progression Unit 4: Personal Development and Innovation	Unit 5: Proposing and Reviewing a Major Project Unit 6: Curating and Presenting a Major Project
UAL (4 units)	Unit 1: Diagnostic Investigation into Creative Practice (Develop knowledge and skills of different art practices)	Units 2 and 3: Developing Specialist Practice (Further exploration, refinement and definition of creative ambitions)	Unit 4: Consolidating Practice (Independent project)

Sources: www.qualifications.pearson.com, www.wjec.co.uk, www.arts.ac.uk
*Ascentis only releases the specification to approved centres.

forget. The Foundation course exhibition might, for example, include static exhibits, multimedia displays and a fashion show.

During the final stage you will be expected to produce a personal confirmatory study or project(s).

Although the three stages are followed by all colleges, tutors have some discretion over the way in which students are taught. There are two main methods. During the exploratory phase, some colleges allocate periods of time to different art and design disciplines, perhaps one week spent on drawing, followed by another on graphics, fine art, fashion, photography and so on. Others prefer to set projects lasting several weeks, which require students to work in several disciplines at the same time.

Students often fall into the trap of assuming that Foundation courses are totally practical. They are not. At least half a day a week will be spent on contextual studies, including the history of art and design, and you will be expected to produce written assignments, including the creation of a personal statement (sometimes known as a statement of intent) that outlines your final major project.

Another common mistake is to think that studying on a Foundation course will be rather like being at school, with free periods during the day. Foundation course students work hard! Many courses will run from Monday to Friday, often from 9.30am to 4.30pm or later, and may include some evening classes. Your working week will be divided into studio practice, lectures and seminars, visits and personal study time. You should ask on an open day what students' daily schedules are like for the course you are interested in.

Although there are exceptions, Foundation courses often have very large numbers of students, sometimes as many as 400, all following the same programme of study. For people used to small class sizes, this prospect can be daunting. In practice, nearly all students find that they quickly adjust to their new working environment. Many students find that they really feed off the hustle and bustle that comes with working in large groups and, in part, the course will be about learning to work with others.

Here are some other characteristics of a Foundation course:

- Do not expect lecturers to spend too much time chasing you up. Making the most of the course will be your responsibility. It will be up to you to attend (and a record of attendance will usually be necessary in order to pass the course).
- You will find yourself involved in group projects and can expect to forge strong friendships with your fellow students.
- The course will be exhausting at times, but it will also be very exciting.

The view of the student set out below should give you more of an idea of what to expect.

> 'What was different about the Foundation course from studying in school was how much more contemporary the approach to art was. All the students were very energetic and enthusiastic about finding something that was interesting and different. Only at the beginning did we make work according to projects, and very quickly we began to create self-directed projects. Every week we would meet for crits to discuss this work. These were central to the course, and if there was one thing that stood out, it was the importance that was given to challenging assumptions of creative decisions; nothing was accepted as self-evident. Discussions were rigorous and the work was often very experimental. This was a challenge because it meant there was not that much support in traditional ways of working. There was not a huge amount of tuition in technique, and the studio was empty when we first arrived; however, it quickly filled with work that was all the more creative and different.
>
> 'Advice I would give would be to be self-directed and to take control in getting as much out of your time on the course as possible (and if you are applying to a Foundation course, it is important to show

that you are this kind of student). You are in a new environment and meeting a lot of new people so it is easy to just accept what is given to you, but part of what you are learning on the Foundation course is to be self-directed; the earlier you can do this, the better. Make a point of getting to know all of the facilities that are available to you; there are likely to be some very skilled technicians in different departments that you can learn a lot from, and they will respond well to enthusiasm that you show. Mix with people from other courses, and don't be held back by an apprehension to experiment or try something different.'

James F, Foundation, Central Saint Martins, Fine Art pathway

Choosing a Foundation course

Getting started

Even though Foundation courses now have a national framework, this may be interpreted very differently by different art schools and colleges, and what suits one student will not be right for another. You can do an initial search on the internet. Have a look at the websites listed in Appendix 1 – the great thing about art schools' and colleges' websites is that they are extremely creative and entertaining. You can spend many happy hours investigating them. They are updated and changed on a regular basis and, at the time of writing, particularly good examples include the University of the Arts London (www.arts.ac.uk), the Architectural Association School of Architecture (www.aaschool.ac.uk), Kingston School of Art (www.kingston.ac.uk), City and Guilds Art School (www.cityandguildsartschool.ac.uk) and Arts University Bournemouth (www.aub.ac.uk).

Next, get hold of as many prospectuses as you can and read them carefully. Do not just look at the pictures, but read about the course structure. If you love photography and this does not seem to feature at a college you are considering, you ought to think twice about applying there.

'I chose Bournemouth for my Foundation because I enjoyed the interview, and because I wanted to be in an art campus as I thought I would prefer being in a creative atmosphere. The tutor was encouraging and I wanted somewhere with a drawing programme as mine was atrocious. I knew I wanted to study fashion for my degree, so the Foundation was a bit frustrating at times as we spent a week on graphics, a week on fashion, and so on. But in retrospect, the skills I learnt doing this were really useful later on in my degree.'

Annabel K, Arts University Bournemouth

Course content

Look very carefully at exactly what you will be able to study. Consider the course content: Is it well structured? Is it flexible enough to allow for personal input? What about the range of subjects covered – is there a wide variety? Although Foundation courses are designed to allow you to gain experience across a whole range of disciplines, they do differ from college to college, and so it is important for you to choose a course that suits your needs. If your aim is to study fashion design at degree level, for example, then you will need to spend at least some of your time specialising in this area of study, so make sure that it is properly catered for.

Location

You can apply anywhere in the country for your Foundation course. However, the majority of students choose somewhere close to home, mostly for practical reasons. These include issues such as accommodation and living expenses, and the reassurance of knowing other people who are at (or have been at) the college. Accommodation, food, travel and materials can be very expensive, and this is a particular issue of concern because a Foundation course is classified as further rather than higher education and you will not be eligible for a student loan. However, UK, Irish and EU students with settled status under 19 years old are not charged tuition fees in further education. (For further information on funding, see Chapter 10.) This is worth remembering, considering the amount you will have to pay for your subsequent course.

It is also worth bearing in mind that Foundation courses are very demanding in terms of time and energy. It is often hard to combine a Foundation course with a part-time job.

There are students who choose to move away from their local area, either because the local college (if there is one) does not suit their preferences or because they want to discover a new environment.

'Year Zero'/Integrated Foundation courses

In Scotland, the usual system is for degree courses in art and design to be four years in length, with the first year being a diagnostic course – the equivalent of a Foundation course. Other institutions elsewhere in the UK also offer this pattern; universities that offer this type of four-year undergraduate degree include: Glasgow School of Art, Norwich University of the Arts, Falmouth and Bath Spa. If you like the idea of continuity – not moving to a different university or college after your first year – you might like to look at this option. There are important funding implications, though. Year Zero students are enrolled on higher education programmes – which makes them liable for tuition fees; you will usually pay the same undergraduate tuition fees as for the other three years. You can find further information on funding in Chapter 10.

Facilities

Questions you may wish to consider include the following.

- How big are the studios?
- Is the light good?
- Will you have your own allocated space, or is it shared?
- What are the IT facilities like?
- Does the college have a well-equipped workshop in which you can experiment with a wide variety of materials?
- Is there a photographic darkroom and studio?
- Will you have access to a ceramics studio?
- Will you have access to specialist studios, or are they exclusive to certain courses?
- What is the library like – is there a wide range of books and a good multimedia section?
- Will you have to pay studio fees, and if so, what will they be? (See Chapter 3 for further information on studio fees.)

You should also think about other issues: what are the communal facilities (such as refectories, bars and social areas) like? Some colleges are attached to universities, and so you might be able to use their facilities as well. However, this might also mean that the social facilities are not on-site, and so some travelling may be necessary.

You will be able to answer some of these questions once you have read the prospectus or looked at the website, but many questions can only be answered by making a visit.

Open days, visits and speaker evenings

It is vital to attend open days or, if this is not possible because the dates clash with other commitments, to arrange a private visit. The facilities and atmosphere of an art college are the key to understanding whether you will be able to flourish there. Whatever the website says, you will only know whether a particular place is right for you by visiting it. Try to talk to current or ex-students to see what they think of the place. Look at the work that has been produced. Does it excite you? Have a good look at the studios. Check out the facilities – are they really as good as they sound? See if the students are working; a successful studio is one in which people are working effectively – is that the case?

Many schools and sixth form colleges organise speaker evenings and other special events in which lecturers, course directors and admissions tutors from local art schools, ex-students and other specialists are invited to talk about what to expect when you study art at institutions of further and higher education. Your local college may also offer a talk as part of its open day. Make sure that you go! Information straight from the horse's mouth can be extremely useful: you get the opportunity to evaluate not only what is being said but also who is saying it and how. Most visiting speakers will try to give you a flavour of the kind of work that you can expect to be involved with. Speakers are usually happy to answer your questions, and they may show you slides or a PowerPoint display to give you an overview of what is on offer. These seminars are extremely useful and are not to be missed.

Even though it is always best to attend in person, many universities offer virtual open days/tours. These allow you to ask questions about the course and facilities, and are a good option for international students who would not otherwise be able to see the university in person.

Atmosphere

Visiting the college is so important because it is the only way to get a feel for its atmosphere. Most people who enjoy art find that the particular qualities of the physical environment and the ambience of the workspace are vital to their creative processes. This varies from person to person, so you will not find league tables ranking colleges in the order of the inspirational effect that they have on their students. Some people like a buzz around them – lots of noise, activity and excitement; others prefer a quieter, more contemplative environment.

How will you know which colleges are right for you? The only way is by visiting them and talking to students who are studying there. Never choose a college solely because someone else, such as a teacher or a parent, says that it would be right for you. Trust your own instincts about whether or not the atmosphere feels right. You are the one who will have to work there!

Making the final selection

Using the considerations covered in this chapter will help you narrow your choice down to a handful of institutions. It is sometimes helpful to rank your shortlist in terms of location, facilities, the course, atmosphere and so on. You could give the top college in each category five points, the second four points and so on. Once you have added up the scores, hopefully some clear winners will emerge. The important thing at this stage is to be honest with yourself about how the colleges match up to your requirements. If a college does not fulfil your needs, then even if going there 'feels' great, it will not be. Make sure that you stick to the criteria and try to establish a clear winner based on the facts. You may well find that a couple of colleges are equally suitable and, at that point, gut feeling may help you to make your decision; but as a general guide, stick to facts and not fiction. In other words, do not believe the hype.

Reputation

Some colleges in the UK are renowned around the world. In some ways, the prestige of these colleges is justified: they attract the most applicants so that they can select the most capable, and this may also be true of the teaching staff as well; they are likely to have good facilities and are located in major cities. As such, you should definitely take a look at them, although gaining entry is very competitive.

However, just because an institution has an excellent reputation, it does not mean that it is necessarily the best fit for you. It is essential not to base your judgement on reputation alone, but to make sure that you gain a good understanding of what studying at these colleges would be like and whether they suit you by visiting them, and other, less well-known colleges. On your visits, consider the emphasis of teaching, the spaces and the attitudes of the staff and students to find the institution most appropriate for you.

Working with your teachers

The final decision on where to go will be yours, but from time to time, we can all benefit from a little guidance. Make sure that you work with your teachers. Talk to them. Ask them what they think your options might be. While no teacher is infallible, they will be able to help. Your teachers will probably have first-hand experience of local Foundation courses and will have some information about application deadlines and portfolio requirements. They will know which of the local courses are the most competitive – and whether you would be in with a chance. (Luckily, since there is no limit to the number of Foundation course applications you can make, you can still have a shot at the most difficult to enter while making one or more other applications for safety.)

It is highly likely that your art teacher will be more closely involved with your application than any other person who teaches you, so make sure that you maintain a good relationship with them and try to take full advantage of their expertise.

> **TIP!**
>
> Try to be organised. You will need to create a file or folder to store all the forms and information you will receive. Make sure that you keep your diary or personal organiser up to date. If you do not use one, now is the time to start. The last thing you want to do is miss out on the chance to visit a college because you forgot the date of the open day. Do not try to keep all of this information in your head – you will not be able to remember everything. Before making your choice, make sure that you also read Chapter 7, 'Putting together a portfolio'.

Entry requirements

As is the case with degree course applications, each institution will have its own entrance requirements for art Foundation courses. These will be specified in the Foundation sections of the colleges' websites. As well as your portfolio of work, most courses will require:

- 3–5 GCSE (or equivalent) passes at Grade 4/C or above, including Mathematics and English;
- 1 A level (or equivalent) pass, usually with one being an art, design or media subject. Other common qualifications include a BTEC in an art and design subject, or an International Baccalaureate.

Institutions may be able to accept students who do not fulfil such requirements under the proviso that they attend classes in these subjects. If you have any doubts about your eligibility, it is best to contact the college/university directly. Information on how to apply for Foundation courses can be found in Chapter 5.

Checklist

- Send off for prospectuses.
- Check out websites.
- Confirm dates for open days, visits and speaker evenings – and attend them.
- Draw up shortlists.
- Talk things through.
- Make a decision.
- Make your application.

3 | Degree courses

This chapter provides an overview of degree courses in art and design. It aims to give you a feel for what to expect at degree level and discusses aspects of how to find the right course for you. Architecture courses are dealt with in Chapter 4.

Where are you now?

By the time Foundation students begin the second term of their course, most, though not all, have a fairly good idea of the direction in which their work is heading. Having completed the exploratory phase of the course in which you experimented with a variety of materials and methods across a broad range of disciplines, you will have chosen a specialist area of study such as fashion, textiles, painting, illustration or product design. By this point you will have begun the process of putting together a portfolio and will be considering your options at degree level. Alternatively, you may be a diploma student in your second year of study.

In both cases, you will have begun to specialise in a particular area of art and design practice and will be considering your options at degree level. In some cases, although rarely, you will be in the second year of your A levels and considering making a direct application to degree courses.

What is a degree course?

An honours degree course is a specialist programme of study offering students the chance to develop practical skills in, and experience and understanding of, a specific area of art and design. Courses offered at degree level will combine practice with theory and, as such, most will require you to undertake some form of contextual studies alongside your practical work. This will vary from institution to institution and may consist of a formally presented illustrated dissertation or some type of multimedia presentation. All courses will show you how to operate within your chosen area of study at a highly sophisticated level. Applications to most degree courses are made through the UCAS system.

Higher National Diploma (HND) courses are generally of two years' duration, and on many HND courses, students have the option of transferring to the bachelor's degree (BA) course.

Honours degree courses usually last for three years. Most of them are self-validating. (This means that the institutions offering them have the power to award their own degrees.) In some cases, however, such as in smaller institutions, the degree is awarded by a university that validates the course on behalf of the college. Do not worry if an institution does not award its own degrees. Some highly respected art schools that have international reputations and recruit students from all over the world do not do so. The college's website will give details of the accrediting university.

Although there are exceptions, within the field of art and design there are three broad areas of study available at degree level, and it is from these that you will select a specialist area of study:

- fine art;
- visual communications and design;
- the applied arts.

Specialisations found within the areas of visual communications and design or the applied arts typically aim to prepare you for the workplace and, in that sense, may be highly vocational in nature. Sometimes they will include a period of work experience. Courses based on fine art, such as painting or sculpture, will be more geared to professional studio practice (although your creative skills may also be valued by industry).

There are essentially four different types of degree you can choose to take: single or joint honours, or a modular or sandwich degree.

Single honours

Most art and design students studying at degree level in the UK follow a single honours course. Competition for places at well-known universities and colleges is strong. You have to compete to get on a degree course, as there are more applicants than places.

In 2024, there were approximately 174,000 applications and only about 30,500 acceptances. UK applicants numbered approximately 139,000, of which about 27,000 (19%) were accepted. International students made some 34,700 applications, of which approximately 3,800 (11%) were accepted.

Courses at colleges with international reputations (and there are many) attract enormous numbers of applications. Places at these institutions are as hard-won as for any other type of undergraduate study. Courses typically run for three years and will require you to complete some form of moderated study of the history of art and design. You will have to pass this element of the course in order to be awarded your degree.

Joint honours and modular degrees

Joint honours courses make it possible to combine the study of distinct but often complementary subjects, such as a BA in Art and Psychology, which is offered by Reading University. Some degrees offer the option to choose from various modules for a portion of the course; these modules may be in a wide range of subjects that are studied alongside art and design. For example, the Fine Art BA course at Central Saint Martins includes a choice of modules as part of the Year 2 Critical Studies programme.

Sandwich degrees

These may be any of the course types mentioned above, but will also contain some form of structured work experience. Most typically this will take the form of a 'year out' beginning at the end of the second year, in which you will work in industry, returning to complete your studies in the fourth and final year. This will normally be arranged by the university.

A year abroad
Some courses provide an opportunity for students to spend a period of time studying overseas. For example, the University of Leeds Fine Art BA course offers the option to extend the course with an extra year studying abroad at a partnered university. For further details, look at the college or university websites.

What can you expect from a degree course?

Because you will be studying for three years or more and will be concentrating your efforts in a specific area of art and design, on a degree course you can expect to develop high levels of expertise. Degree courses should offer you excellent facilities and technical support within your chosen area and will also provide you with access to resources outside your specialisation, often by means of reciprocal arrangements with other institutions. You will be asked to consider issues and ideas at their most fundamental level and encouraged to fully realise your creative potential. You can expect to enjoy the full range of extracurricular activities that are available to all undergraduates.

Entry requirements

- The Course Search facility on the UCAS website provides links to all degree courses and includes information on entry requirements. This will be given in terms of A level grades, International Baccalaureate, Scottish Highers and most recognised international qualifications. Entry requirements may also be given as a score on the UCAS Tariff – a system of allocating points to academic qualifications. However, for almost all creative courses, a portfolio

of work will be the main means of assessment. The university or college will specify that 'for the first year entry of this course, you will be assessed by portfolio/evidence.'
- Information on the UCAS Tariff can be found at www.ucas.com/undergraduate/what-and-where-study/entry-requirements/ucas-tariff-points.

Degree course specialisations

There is an enormously wide variety of specialist courses available at degree level (see Figure 3). Some disciplines will be familiar to you; others will be entirely new.

Taking the three general areas of study already mentioned as a starting point, the following lists are designed to give an overview of some of the courses available. These lists are not definitive – new courses are being set up every year. Please note that some specialist areas of study appear in more than one list. This is because a subject such as photography, for example, could be studied in the context of fine art, with an emphasis placed on personal self-expression, or might be offered as a visual communications course if it concentrates on preparing you for a career in photojournalism.

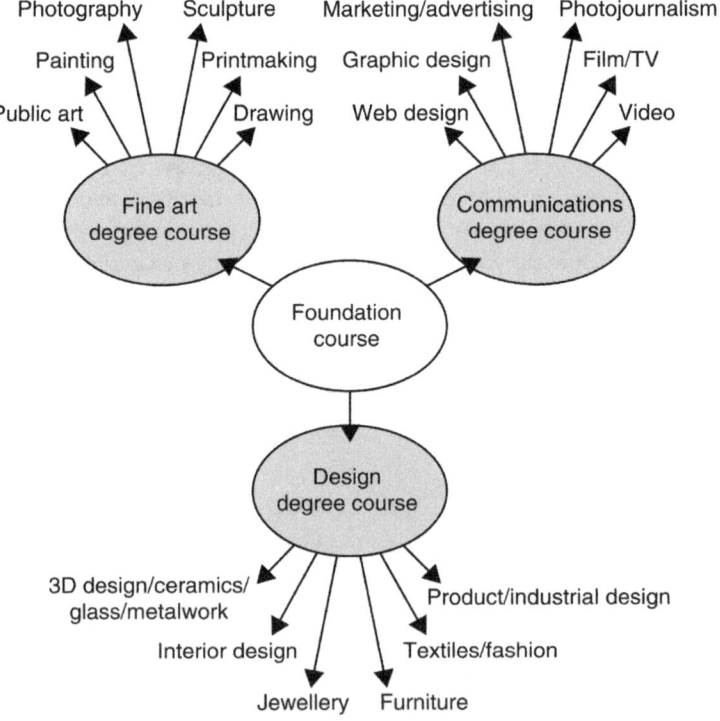

Figure 3 Specialist courses

Fine art

These courses, which place an emphasis on personal creativity and self-expression, can cover a wide variety of disciplines and often include:

- conceptual art;
- drawing;
- painting;
- photography and film;
- printmaking;
- sculpture.

Visual communications

These courses are typically vocational and can sometimes include a period of work experience:

- advertising;
- animation;
- commercial photography;
- creative computing;
- design for publishing;
- fashion communication and promotion;
- fashion marketing;
- fashion photography;
- film and television;
- graphic design;
- illustration;
- photography;
- print and graphic communication;
- typographic design;
- virtual reality.

Design and the applied arts

Again, these courses are usually vocational in nature and often aim to prepare students for professional practice:

- architectural glass;
- ceramics;
- conservation;
- fashion;
- furniture;
- games art and design;
- games development;
- glass;
- interaction design;
- interior design;
- jewellery;
- knitwear design;
- museum and exhibition design;
- performance costume;
- product design;
- silversmithing;
- textiles;
- theatre: designing for performance;
- user experience design;
- visual effects.

Foundation degrees

So far, we have been talking about honours degrees, but there is another type of degree course available that you might like to consider.

Foundation degrees have been available since 2001 and are on offer in a wide range of subjects. The title is a little unfortunate since they could easily be confused with Foundation courses! The new courses are a qualification in their own right and can also lead on to an honours degree course. Designed in consultation with employers, they are courses that train people in specialist career areas and develop:

- work skills relevant to a particular careers area;
- key skills, for example, communication and problem-solving;
- general skills, such as reasoning and professionalism.

If you do a Foundation degree, you will be able to choose between entering employment and continuing training in your job, or converting the qualification into an honours degree through further study, usually by transfer into the second or third year of a related degree course. Foundation degrees are available in a range of disciplines, including graphics, fashion, product and furniture design, game art and design, CGI and visual effects, hair and make-up and interior and architectural design. A full list of courses and more information can be found in the Foundation degree section on the UCAS website (www.ucas.com).

Degree apprenticeships

The vocational higher education market is growing in the UK, with more emphasis placed on teaching practical skills alongside qualifications, with a view to addressing the high-level skills gap that exists in certain industries. This allows for the combination of full-time paid employment with part-time study, enabling students to have the benefit of experiencing both work and study. Art and design technology are common fields that lend themselves well to degree apprenticeships. There are currently over 60 universities implementing degree apprenticeships in the UK and the number of employers signing up to the scheme is growing.

Some examples of degree apprenticeships

- architecture;
- automotive design;
- product design.

How much will a degree apprenticeships cost? Nothing. Employers are expected to cover the cost of apprenticeship training. This will, however, mean more competition for places. NB: You are not guaranteed a job at the end of a degree apprenticeships, but you will be guaranteed to be employable within a skills-based sector, which will give you a significant advantage. Consult www.prospects.ac.uk/jobs-and-work-experience/apprenticeships/degree-apprenticeships and www.ucas.com/apprenticeships/degree-apprenticeships for more information.

It is also possible to gain apprenticeships in ceramics, costume and wardrobe, fashion and textiles, jewellery and photography but these are often offered at a lower level.

Finding the right course

Most students applying for places on specialist degree courses either are attending or have been to art school. Perhaps you have been studying close to home and want to move further afield, or perhaps you are well established where you are. You may have a pretty good idea of what you are looking for, but try to keep an open mind. Do your homework. Get hold of as many prospectuses as you can and read them carefully. Don't just look at the pictures; read about the course structure and content. If you plan to study furniture design, for example, and love to make things in the workshop, make sure that the courses you are considering are supportive of this approach. Use the internet – the great thing about art schools' and colleges' websites is that they are extremely creative and entertaining. Information on how to apply for undergraduate courses can be found in Chapter 5.

Course content

How will you know which course is going to suit you? For example, what is the difference between studying a BA in Glass and a BA in Architectural Glass? Degree courses in specific subjects will differ from college to college. Some illustration courses, for instance, will place more emphasis on digital manipulation while others will focus more on traditional drawing techniques – so it is important for you to understand exactly what is being offered.

Take full advantage of the literature available. Make sure that you read and fully comprehend the course specification. If you are unclear about anything, try to speak to the course director or head of school. Look very carefully at exactly what will be studied, at what point in the course and for how long and how much flexibility and choice you will have. For example, if you want to become a forensic photographer, make sure that you are not applying to a fine art photography course!

Since many art and design graduates work freelance, it is important for them to understand how to run their own business – about finding premises to work in, tax and legal requirements and how to calculate costs when pricing their work – and how to market their work and present it to prospective employers or buyers. If you think you may freelance in the future, ask now whether the course contains modules on self-employment, given either by course tutors or by the college or university careers service.

> 'I can still remember the day I got my offer from Chelsea College of Art for the BA in Textiles design. All the effort I had put into my studies at MPW had paid off.
>
> 'I had always been told that university involved a great deal of independent practice and the ability to complete multiple projects

at once is the most important and basic skill. In the beginning, I was worried about the sudden change of unsupervised learning and how that might be difficult, but my experience at Chelsea was that, although the work is self-motivated, this gave me the chance to discover my passions and push myself out of my comfort zone.

'The tutors and technicians were very responsible and engaged; they have rich experience and knowledge in their field and always provide guidance according to the preferences of each student.

'Over the three years, I learnt lots of new skills: the use of domestic and industrial knitting machines, stitch techniques, embroidery, weaving, printing; and we always had the opportunity to get knowledge from the other subjects to enrich our own practice.

'Thinking and solving problems was a huge learning curve, but having peers to discuss ideas with was priceless.'

Jess Z, BA Textiles with Knit, Chelsea College of Art

Location

You can apply anywhere in the country, or even abroad, for your degree course. Consider the practicalities of your course location, such as the cost of accommodation and travel. Moving to a big city may be attractive, but will you be able to afford it? Many students enjoy and benefit from the dynamism that city life can offer; some prefer to live and work in a quieter location. What will be right for you? For many students, it is essential that they are close to galleries and museums. What are the local facilities like? Do they meet your needs? Higher education is expensive, and although you may get some financial help, nearly all students have to raise funds privately. If you are planning to work part-time, are there job opportunities?

'My time at New York University was truly transformative. The dynamic atmosphere and innovative approach to arts education in the NYU Studio Art programme provided me with a unique and enriching experience. The talented faculty and diverse student community fostered a creative environment that encouraged exploration and pushed boundaries. The influence of New York City goes far beyond the classroom, and not only has it left an enduring imprint on my artistic prowess but it has also significantly shaped my perspective on the world.'

Adam G, BA, New York University

Facilities

Does the college have the facilities that you will need to study your subject? A degree course studio should be very well equipped. Make sure that the relevant technology is up to date and kept that way. As well as working within your own field, you may well need to cross over into other areas of art and design. Many art schools have reciprocal arrangements with other institutions. Do these exist and will they be practical? If, for example, you intend to study sculpture, you will no doubt be looking for spacious, well-lit and well-equipped studios, but what about the IT facilities? Remember that you will have to put together some kind of contextual study. Are the computers up to the job, and could you use them to create 'virtual' sculpture?

As your skills develop, so will your needs. Try asking yourself the question: 'Do I know what all the equipment is for?' If you do, then the course is probably not well equipped.

You should also think about communal facilities such as refectories, bars and social areas. Some colleges are attached to universities, and so you might be able to use their facilities as well. However, this might also mean that the social facilities are not on-site and so some travelling may be necessary.

Student support

Does the institution provide good welfare arrangements, such as student counsellors and an accommodation office?

Additional costs

Your tuition fees are unlikely to cover all of the costs of materials that will be needed for the course; these include art materials, printing and other costs essential to the course. The course website will often give details about the extra costs you can expect; most universities describe these as being around £350–£500 per year, and may be higher in the final year.

Some institutions may charge students studio fees, which are fees paid to the university for some of the costs of materials and facilities; these can vary considerably from place to place. If the course you are considering does have these fees, it is worth finding out what the fees are and what facilities you get for the money (this is not always set out in prospectuses or course leaflets). You could also check – perhaps by asking a student on an open day – whether the final degree show involves students in much expenditure. You will be able to answer some of these questions once you have read the prospectus or looked at the website, but many questions can be answered only by making a visit.

Open days and visits

It is only by visiting a department that you will get a feel for its atmosphere. Most artists and designers find that the physical environment and the ambience of the workspace are vital to their creative processes. This varies from person to person, so you will not find league tables ranking colleges in the order of the inspirational effect they have on their students. But ask yourself: 'What is the vibe like?' It might suit other people, but will it suit you? Make a point of talking to students who are studying there. Is the working environment a productive one? Can you picture yourself in it? Never choose a college solely because someone else says that it would be right for you. Trust your own instincts about whether or not the atmosphere feels right. After all, you are the one who is going to study there!

If you are an international student visiting the UK, it may be worth arranging a private tour, as many institutions can arrange this. Otherwise, book a place on one of the published open days or virtual open days.

Past students

It is always interesting to look at the names of practising artists who have graduated from the university or art school. Although famous alumni do not necessarily make one institution better than another, they can act as a guide to the type of work that is being undertaken there. And if an artist you really admire studied on one of the courses you are investigating, this can add to the attraction of the college.

The final choice

Remember that you are going to have to live with this decision for three or four years, so try not to be carried away by a sudden rush of blood to the head. As important as it is to trust your instincts, using the steps outlined above to narrow down your choice to a handful of institutions will help you make a decision you won't regret.

Go through this list and think things over carefully. Talk things through with the people who know you best – you will benefit from a second opinion. Rank your shortlist in terms of location, facilities, the course, atmosphere and so on. Try giving the top course in each category five points, the second four points and so on. Use the scores to help identify which course meets your requirements. You will probably find that there are two or three courses that are up there. Don't be afraid to trust your instincts, but make sure that your shortlist is based in reality and not fantasy. Read the views below on making that final choice.

> *'I'm in my final year of BA Interior and Spatial Design at Chelsea College of Arts, and honestly, it's been a mix of exhaustion, excitement and growth. The course constantly pushes you to think differently, not just about how a space looks, but how it feels and what story it tells. During my first two years, I worked on projects that explored design methods, materiality and collaboration, and now in my final year, I'm developing two projects that feel deeply personal.*
>
> *'There were times I felt completely lost, especially in the first year, when everyone seemed to already know so much about software and design theory. I've had weeks where I barely slept trying to*

perfect a project before deadlines (terrible idea, please don't do that). If I've learned anything, it's that time management and self-care matter more than perfection.

'Chelsea has such a creative atmosphere; tutors genuinely care and always encourage us to explore our own direction. We visit museums, exhibitions and design studios all the time, which really shapes your perspective as a designer. If you're thinking of applying, try to learn a bit of Rhino, SketchUp, AutoCAD, Photoshop or InDesign beforehand, it'll save you a lot of stress. It's not been easy, but I wouldn't trade it for anything. Every project, every challenge has made me more confident, curious and sure that this is what I'm meant to do.'

Alina K, BA Interior and Spatial Design,
Chelsea College of Arts

'I am currently studying the BA Jewellery Design course at the University of Arts London – Central Saint Martins. My journey into this field began during my A levels, fuelled by a deep fascination with gems and stones. Beyond their inherent preciousness and beauty, I am fond of their intricate structures and how they seamlessly integrate into jewellery pieces. Transitioning from my initial fascination with aesthetics, I have come to understand that jewellery design is beyond mere ornamentation; it encapsulates profound concepts and pursues a commitment to environmental sustainability. My A level aspirations to secure a spot in the BA Jewellery Design course were not just about education; they were the foundation for my ambition to establish my own brand and business. Designing jewellery has proven to me it transcends a creative endeavour; it requires responsibility, discipline, commitment and the ability to be innovative, qualities that drove my pursuit of realising my ambitions.'

Saroushka L, BA Jewellery Design,
Central St Martins

'Studying at Central Saint Martins was like riding a creative rollercoaster. On my BA Textiles Design course, I dove into print, where every project was a new chance to play with patterns and colours. The place buzzed with energy, and it was all about trying out wild ideas and seeing what stuck. Now, on my MA Material Futures course, things are getting even cooler. It's like exploring uncharted territory, mixing up tech and eco-friendly vibes. The whole experience is more like hanging out in an artist's dream lab than sitting in a classroom. I am making some great mates, laughing a lot and picking up a whole new perspective on design. It isn't just about getting a degree; it is about growing into a more creative, chilled-out version of myself. I can't wait to see where this journey takes me next.'

May M, MA Material Futures Art,
Central St Martins

'As a current Year 1 student at London College of Communication (LCC) on the BA Animation course, I am satisfied with the experience so far. University offers a range of useful facilities, from access to libraries or studios with computers and drawing tablets, to various software, including Toon Boom and Autodesk Maya, which are industry-standard in animation production. Tutors and lecturers have experience in industry, and can often answer questions related to finding work placements. We get a lot of help, especially from our head of department.

'However, it is a place for those who are ready to learn independently. Briefs, explanations and instructions are always given at the beginning of every project. While students are welcome to ask any question regarding upcoming projects, the university expects almost full independence from students, the ability to use given materials and learn on their own. This helps to develop creative thinking, but may not suit some students.

'Overall, I made a great choice to study in LCC, and am looking forward to many exciting animation projects in the future.'

Dariga A, BA Animation, London College of Communication

'I'm currently studying in my first year of a BA in Fashion Design at the University of Edinburgh. So far, I have already learnt so much about pattern cutting and constructing garments. The course is very creative and allows you to go in your own direction, but also focuses largely on skills and pattern cutting; this is great, as being able to create patterns and make garments is a very useful skill to have in the fashion industry. I highly recommend this course to anyone wanting to study fashion design as it teaches you a wide range of skills that will prepare you well for life after university.'

Honor H, BA Fashion Design, University of Edinburgh

Checklist

- Send off for prospectuses.
- Check out prospectuses, university guides and so on.
- Check out websites.
- Confirm dates for open days, visits and speaker evenings – and attend them.
- Talk to tutors.
- Draw up shortlists.
- Talk things through.
- Make a decision.
- Make your application.

4| Architecture

There are a number of possible routes for students who wish to apply for architecture courses. Applications for some courses, such as those offered by art colleges, are made in the same way as for other art and design courses; but you can also apply to study architecture at university without the need to do a Foundation course, or at private institutions. These routes are described in this chapter.

Of all the different manifestations of art and design that we encounter in our daily lives, the work of architects is, along with that of clothes and product designers, the one that people come into contact with most often. Every shop, office building, fast-food outlet, cinema, bridge or multi-storey car park that you see on your way to school or work has been designed by an architect. The work of some architects is immediately recognisable: London's 'Gherkin' and The Shard, Paris's Pompidou Centre or Bilbao's Guggenheim museum spring to mind. But your home was also designed by an architect, as was your train or bus station.

To practise as an architect in the UK, you need to gain registration with the Architects Registration Board (ARB). This takes a minimum of seven years after you leave school. But don't be put off by this if you are interested in architecture because this does not mean that you will spend seven years in lectures; although you will have to attend some lectures, the seven years involve a combination of academic study and work experience in an architectural practice. If you are interested in architecture and want a shorter course so that you can work within the fields of architecture or related subjects such as interior design, then there are other, shorter options available. This chapter will explain the different routes available to you.

Qualifying as an architect

Registration with the ARB

In order to gain registration with the ARB, you need to pass three stages, which are overseen by the Royal Institute of British Architects (RIBA – incidentally, if you are serious about becoming an architect, try to visit the RIBA's London headquarters, which holds many exhibitions as well as being home to an impressive architecture bookshop). A typical route to gaining registration is shown in Table 2 (overleaf).

Table 2 Typical registration route

Year	Programme	Stage in the RIBA Process
1, 2, 3	Bachelor's degree in architecture – BA, BArch, BSc or equivalent	Part 1
4	Work experience	
5, 6	Postgraduate study – Dip Arch, MArch or equivalent	Part 2
7	Hold RIBA Part 1 and Part 2 and have at least two years' work experience (12 months of this experience should be in a UK/EU practice). Professional Practice examination	Part 3

Choosing a course

If you are going to embark on the journey towards becoming an architect, you need to think carefully about the first three years of the course. There are a number of options and the right one for you will depend very much on your academic and creative strengths. There are about 74 universities in the UK that offer three- or four-year undergraduate degrees in architecture (usually UCAS code K100 or K101) that will give you exemption from RIBA Part 1. There is a section on the RIBA website that lists these institutions (see Chapter 12). Some of these are more geared towards students who are interested in the structural as well as the creative aspects of architecture, and these often require A levels in Mathematics and/or Physics.

Other universities concentrate more on the creative aspects of architecture and so require an A level in Art. In some cases, history of art can be an advantage if the course has a significant focus on the historical side of architecture. You will often hear people talking about 'the language of architecture'; in the same way that there are rules – which of course can be broken – governing the construction of sentences when we speak English, architects use architectural elements in the design of buildings. Some of these are new, but often they are based on historical ideas. Just as we mix old and new words in a sentence, architects can mix old and new architectural details in a building. For entry onto these courses, you will be judged on your portfolio as well as on your academic achievements or predictions. In addition to the above entry requirements, some universities also set a practical task.

If you are reading this before choosing your A level (or equivalent) subjects, then spend some time looking at the entrance requirements of university architecture courses to ensure that you will have the right subjects to apply for the type of course that will suit you best. If you are already studying A levels, then you still need to do this research to ensure that you do not waste choices on your UCAS application. The UCAS website 'Course Search' facility is a good starting place, as the list of K100/K101 architecture courses has links through to the universities' entrance requirements. If you are already studying A levels and you are not doing the right subjects for an application to study architecture, you have two options.

- Take an extra year on your A levels, and add the necessary subjects. Some further education colleges and a number of independent sixth form colleges will offer a fast-track one-year A level programme.
- Think about following an Access course or an art Foundation course. The universities will be able to advise you on what alternatives to A levels they might be prepared to accept.

Entry requirements

When looking at entry requirements for architecture courses, you should be aware that while these will specify particular grades or scores at A level, International Baccalaureate, Scottish Highers or international qualifications, the universities will also be looking at the following.

- Is the candidate genuinely interested in, and suitable for, architecture?
- Is the candidate doing the right subjects?

Some universities will also set an additional entrance test or creative task in order to assess the applicant's creativity.

> **WARNING!**
>
> Do not assume that if a university requires, for example, AAA at A level and you are confident of achieving these grades, this guarantees a place. You would first have to get an offer of a place (either conditional upon achieving the grades, or an unconditional offer if you have already achieved the grades).

Diploma courses

An alternative to the university route described above is offered by the Architectural Association (AA) School of Architecture in London. The AA is, as its name suggests, a specialist architecture school, and it offers a Foundation course for students with a limited art background, a three-year course leading to RIBA Part 1 and diploma and master's courses for students wishing to qualify as architects or to pursue postgraduate studies in architecture.

For entry to the Foundation course, students can apply with one A level at A*–C. If you apply with only one A level, it must be in a non-art/design subject. So, you cannot apply with an A* in Art and Design or Product Design or similar. You must also provide your GCSE certificates or the equivalent for study in Year 10/11 (this is usually grade 9–10 if you are an overseas student). Please note, EU and international students without settled or pre-settled status will have to apply for a visa after they have been offered their place on the course. More information can be found on page 64.

Preparation for your application

Architecture courses are oversubscribed. For 2024 entry, according to UCAS, there were around 5,600 places available for architecture and 35,000 applicants; so, it is important to be able to demonstrate to the admissions staff that you are a serious applicant. For 2024 entry, UK students numbered 25,700 with 4,700 acceptances. For international students, the figures are even less encouraging. For 2024 entry, around 900 international students (of about 9,600 applicants) gained places.

In order to make your application as strong as possible, other things you should do prior to the application include:

- reading books on the history of architecture, and on contemporary architecture;
- doing some research on the uses of, and properties of, common building materials such as glass, steel, concrete, stone and so on.;
- background reading on a favourite building or structure (preferably one you have visited);
- visiting exhibitions;
- keeping a small notebook with you, in which you can make notes and sketches of buildings that interest you.

And, of course, all these things will be mentioned in your UCAS personal statement. See below and Chapter 5 for more details.

Alternative architecture courses

Not everyone who has an interest in studying architecture wants to practice as an architect. There are a whole range of other careers that involve architecture, including:

- administration work in an architectural practice;
- local council planning;
- architectural model-making or computer-aided design;
- architectural photographer;
- interior design;
- structural engineering;
- teaching.

There are several courses other than the K100 degrees mentioned in the previous section that can lead to careers associated with architecture. For example:

- courses at art schools, such as the three-year BA in Interior Architecture and Design at Arts University Bournemouth or the BA in Interior and Spatial Design at Camberwell College of Arts;
- engineering-related courses, such as structural or architectural engineering;
- art history courses.

Entry onto some courses may require the student to have completed an Art Foundation course (see Chapter 2).

The personal statement

A personal statement for entry onto an architecture course should incorporate the following sections.

- Why do you want to study this course?
- How have your qualifications and studies helped you to prepare for this course?
- What else have you done to prepare outside of education and why are these experiences useful?

Remember, the personal statement is limited to 4,000 characters.

Personal statement 1 - Architecture degree application

Why do you want to study this course or subject?

My fascination with structures and spaces began in childhood, when I spent hours building Lego® creations. What started as play – turning small, colourful blocks into towers, vehicles or machines – sparked a lasting curiosity about how parts come together to form something greater. As I grew older, I realised it wasn't just the act of building that inspired me, but the creativity and problem-solving behind it: how structures shape experiences, reflect ideas and respond to people's needs. Architecture, to me, is both an art form and a social responsibility, one that captures history, identity and imagination in physical form.

Travel and exposure to different cultures have deepened this fascination. Observing how geography, tradition and innovation influence architectural styles has shown me that buildings are more than physical constructs; they are reflections of civilisation and human progress. Architecture tells stories about the people who design and inhabit spaces, and I am determined to become one of those storytellers.

How have your qualifications and studies helped you to prepare for this course or subject?

My A level subjects – Mathematics, Physics and Art & Design – have given me a strong foundation for studying architecture. Mathematics has developed my problem-solving and analytical skills; Physics has helped me understand structure, materials and natural forces; and Art has allowed me to explore creativity, form and visual communication. Working across these disciplines has taught me to balance logic with imagination, precision with freedom.

Beyond my studies, I challenge myself through drawing and model-making. I experiment with pencils, markers, clay, wire mesh and copper wire to transform concepts into three-dimensional forms. This process has strengthened my patience, spatial awareness and understanding of composition and scale. I am particularly interested in how materials and light influence the emotional response to space.

What else have you done to prepare outside of education, and why are these experiences useful?

My work experience placements confirmed my desire to pursue architecture professionally. At Map Projects in London, I attended site meetings, observed client negotiations and took part in design discussions that revealed how collaboration and iteration drive architectural practice. At Dewan Architects in Dubai, I followed projects from concept through development, observing sustainability strategies and material selection. Speaking with architects at various stages of their careers gave me valuable insight into the realities and rewards of the profession and strengthened my determination to enter the field.

I am curious, reflective and motivated; qualities I believe are essential for both study and practice. Visiting universities and engaging with tutors and students has reinforced my enthusiasm and helped me identify the kind of creative, studio-based environment in which I will thrive. I am eager to learn how design can improve lives, strengthen communities and respond sensitively to environmental challenges.

Studying architecture will allow me to combine my analytical strengths with my artistic interests, and to contribute ideas that unite function, innovation and beauty. I am fully committed to developing the skills, discipline and creativity required to become an architect, and I look forward to exploring the endless possibilities that architecture offers to shape a better, more inspiring world.

Personal statement 2 - Architecture degree application

Why do you want to study this course or subject?

My interest in architecture began in childhood when I spent hours constructing toy buildings and sculptures. I was drawn to toys that gave me the freedom to create whatever I imagined. This fascination with form and structure grew into a passion for design, particularly how creativity and function merge to shape the spaces we live in.

A formative moment came during a choir tour in Barcelona when I visited Parc Güell. I was captivated by Gaudí's ability to draw inspiration from nature and translate organic forms into striking structures. His imaginative use of shape and texture inspired me to explore the wider Art Nouveau movement.

Exploring the influence of Art Nouveau led me to Art Deco, where I discovered a different kind of beauty: symmetry, precision and geometric rhythm. I was fascinated by how Art Deco merged modernity with ancient symbolism, creating something both progressive and timeless. This progression between styles deepened my understanding of how architecture continuously evolves while echoing its cultural roots.

How have your qualifications and studies helped you to prepare for this course or subject?

Growing up in Tehran, surrounded by dense urban development, I often felt the loss of cultural identity in many new constructions. Through my A level in Art and Design and my introductory architectural studies, I was introduced to Thiis-Evensen's writings on phenomenology in architecture. These studies helped me understand how built environments can shape human experience beyond their material form, allowing me to analyse my own surroundings with greater critical awareness. The contrast between authenticity and imitation that I observed, now understood through the theoretical frameworks I studied, pushed me to think deeply about architecture's cultural and emotional responsibilities.

My research projects in A level Geography and Environmental Design further shaped my outlook. Studying the ancient city of Yazd, I examined its ingenious wind chimneys, or badgirs, which naturally cool interior spaces. Learning about these systems in an academic context helped me appreciate how sustainable thinking has long been part of architectural tradition. I believe modern cities could learn from such environmentally responsive designs, something I hope to explore further through my architectural studies.

Through my A level work in Fine Art, and particularly after visiting Rachel Whiteread's exhibition on negative space, I learned to see form and absence differently. Her work prompted me to investigate how architecture can be defined not only by structure but by the voids within it. I experimented with photography to explore similar ideas in two dimensions, capturing shadows and outlines that suggest unseen spaces. These creative explorations have strengthened my ability to observe, interpret and conceptualise spatial relationships, all of which prepare me for studying architecture at a higher level.

What else have you done to prepare outside of education, and why are these experiences useful?

My practical experience has also deepened my understanding of structure and design. I worked one day a week for a year at a structural engineering company, where I observed how technical and creative decisions intersect in real projects. I also helped teach a workshop on tensegrity models, which strengthened my grasp of balance, tension and compression while improving my leadership and communication skills.

As vice president and information officer of my school's student council, I have organised charity events, led meetings and supported younger students through a debating club. These experiences have developed my teamwork, organisation and confidence; all qualities that I know are vital in architecture school and beyond.

I am drawn to architecture because it unites creativity, science and cultural meaning. I want to design spaces that are not only functional and beautiful but also rooted in place, history and human experience. I am committed to studying architecture because it offers the perfect balance of artistic expression, technical challenge and the opportunity to contribute meaningfully to the built environment.

Personal statement 3 - Architecture degree application

Why do you want to study this course or subject?

My passion for architecture began with the creative freedom it offers and the joy it brings to others. Over time, this passion has evolved into a deeper awareness of the significance of architecture in shaping our environment and the powerful role it plays in improving cities and communities. I am especially intrigued by how architectural design can respond to the challenges of climate change. Architects such as Laurie Baker have inspired me through their sustainable and context-sensitive approaches. His work, like the Centre for Development Studies, demonstrates his philosophy that 'architecture should merge with the surrounding landscape, rather than compete with it'. His principles highlight how thoughtful design can harmonise with nature rather than dominate it.

As someone of Ethiopian heritage, I have long been surrounded by examples of vernacular and biophilic architecture that embody this same respect for the natural environment. Visits to the Dorze region allowed me to witness traditional building methods that use local and renewable materials such as grass, bamboo and banana leaves. The rounded, organic forms of these huts, shaped like beehives or elephant heads, reflect a deep connection to nature and its preservation. Observing these practices helped me realise that the most sustainable designs are often the most practical and contextually suited, reaffirming Baker's belief that 'cost-effective hours are not always for the poor.'

How have your qualifications and studies helped you to prepare for this course or subject?

My studies in art have heightened my awareness of the environmental crises that modern architecture must respond to. I became particularly interested in the work of Koen Olthuis, whose floating structures propose a visionary response to rising sea levels. Inspired by his ideas, I applied my knowledge of physics to explore how buoyancy, balance and energy efficiency influence design. I investigated tensegrity platforms; elegant systems of tension and compression that maintain equilibrium regardless of weight distribution. This research helped me understand how scientific principles can offer sustainable solutions in architectural innovation.

I also examined the material properties of cedar wood as a potential alternative for beams and cladding. Its lightness, weather resistance and dimensional stability make it both energy-efficient and environmentally friendly. Through this exploration, I discovered the importance of selecting materials that not only serve a structural purpose but also reflect ecological responsibility. These experiments deepened my appreciation of how design, physics and environmental awareness can intersect to create practical and sustainable architecture.

What else have you done to prepare outside of education, and why are these experiences useful?

My work experience at AM Meri Architecture Firm strengthened this understanding by allowing me to observe how professional architects apply sustainable practices in real-world projects. I gained insight into how designs evolve from concept to execution and how environmental, social and structural considerations must coexist in every stage of development.

These experiences have solidified my ambition to study architecture and contribute to shaping a more sustainable future. I am particularly motivated by the possibilities of designing adaptable and environmentally responsive structures; ideas that have given me hope for the future of both architecture and human life on Earth.

I believe that my curiosity, determination and respect for the natural world will allow me to thrive in the demanding yet rewarding study of architecture. I look forward to learning from experts, developing my creative and technical abilities and contributing innovative ideas that align with the urgent environmental needs of our time. For me, architecture is more than the design of buildings; it is a means of harmonising humanity with nature, ensuring that our structures sustain rather than deplete the world we inhabit.

You will have noticed that the applicants have dropped a number of hints as to what they would like to discuss at the interview, by mentioning ideas, buildings and architects. If they are lucky, the interviewer will be interested in hearing them expand on these topics, and so they will be able to talk about things they have already prepared. For example, they have mentioned:

- colour;
- architecture and civilisation;
- 3D modelling;
- use of materials;
- work experience.

In order to impress the interviewer, they would need to do a good deal of research into the things they have touched on in the statement. If there is one thing guaranteed to create a bad impression at the interview, it is being unable to talk about things in the personal statement.

> 'I'm an architecture student at Central Saint Martins. In my experience, working in an arts-focused university has helped me push myself to compete creatively with other students. I've made friends from other courses who give me different perspectives on both my current projects and their designs and proposals. The environment at the university helps us to create a wider conversation with each other about the problems popping up globally, be they political or environmental. I would say the greatest experience I've had at this university has been the allowance of failure, because it has enabled me to adjust my angles of approach to the problem at hand and helped me grow. This road is hard however, and it means you will have to have the drive to push forward and succeed, no matter the disappointments that may set you back.'
>
> Nikan A, BA Architecture, Central Saint Martins

> 'My journey to architecture simply started with drawing in my free time. During A level Art, my interest and passion towards architecture drastically increased. With the help of my tutors, I was able to produce artworks of an exceptional standard that led to an astonishing portfolio and offers from most of my university choices. I chose the AA because of its richness in experimentation, concept and processes. The first year taught us the fundamentals of architecture: how to draw plans, sections, create 3D models and produce architectural diagrams to convey our research and ideas such that the quantity of information delivered is not overwhelming to the viewer. As our tutors always used to tell us: "Quality over quantity", and "Make sure a 10-year-old can understand what you are trying to convey. Only then will your project be successful." I joined an experimental unit in my second year, where the brief was to design a mixed-use high-rise tower with a set of programs of my choosing. I chose a labyrinth of casinos. I particularly enjoyed that year and it opened my eyes when I realised almost any crazy/fictional idea can be developed architecturally. I am

now in the third year, where the experimental brief is to design a museum or a series of them along the OXCAM arc, working through site-selection, context and providing for what's needed – another level of excitement and joy unravelled. History and technical studies sweeten the course even more. Architecture is an incredible field. Let your imagination pave your path.'

Abdullah K, BA Architecture, Architectural Association School of Architecture

'The AA has two identifiable and unique strengths: an embrace of the use of a vast assortment of method and media within projects and an all-encompassing holistic approach to architectural education. It exemplifies the term "association". A community in which students, tutors, lecturers, workshop assistants and librarians can come together, cooperating in the synthesis of ideas.

'You might not know everyone, yet the sense of belonging to a single, unified body of creative minds is ever-present.'

Nazar E, BA Architecture, Architectural Association School of Architecture

> **WARNING!**
>
> Do not copy any of the personal statements in this book: they are only intended to be a guide. You might be tempted to get external help in writing the personal statement. While you should get advice from as many people as you can, you should not get someone else to write it for you or use Artificial Intelligence (AI) software. There are websites that offer (for a fee) to prepare the personal statement for you, but be aware that UCAS uses sophisticated anti-plagiarism software to check each statement, and if it detects that the work is not your own, your application may be cancelled.

Graduate employment

The Higher Education Statistics Agency (HESA) collects data on what graduates do after they have completed their studies. Data collected for the 2022/23 academic year shows that for students who studied architecture, building and planning, 87% of those who responded to the survey were in some form of employment and 13% were involved in some form of further study, including those working and studying.

Source: www.hesa.ac.uk.

5 | How to apply

This chapter explains the procedures for applying for Foundation, degree and Higher National Diploma (HND) courses. However, before you apply, you need to do lots of preparation. If you have not already done so, you should read the relevant sections on choosing a course in Chapters 2, 3 and 4.

Foundation courses

In most cases, you apply directly to the art colleges for entry to their Foundation courses, and you can apply to a number of colleges simultaneously, since there is no central application scheme.

The application forms vary from college to college. All require basic details about yourself and your education, but they differ in the amount of space (if any) that you have to write about yourself and your interests – that is, the personal statement.

Unlike the UCAS scheme for applications to degree courses, there is not one date by which all applications must be submitted. The closing date for applications varies from college to college, and so, you must do your research early and make sure that you do not miss any deadlines. The closing date for applications is often the end of January, but this is not true for all colleges, so consult the prospectus or the website well in advance.

Most Foundation course applications need to be accompanied by a reference, usually from the head teacher or head of art at your school or college. If you are a mature student or are not studying art at school, you should read the 'Non-standard applications' section in this chapter. Warn the person you choose to do the reference well in advance that you are going to apply, and ask them whether they are willing to act as a referee. References usually take time to write, so do not surprise your referee with a form the day before the deadline. Even if he or she does manage to write it in time, it is less likely to be full of the necessary detail, and it will certainly not emphasise your planning and organisational skills!

Bear in mind that you are applying for a place on a practical course, so the application form is only the starting point. The key elements of the selection process are the portfolio and/or the interview. Admissions staff will place most emphasis on evidence of high potential and creative ability. See Chapters 7 and 8 for more information. If your initial application is successful, you will be asked to deliver (or send) your portfolio to the college so that it can be assessed by the selectors, or to attend an interview at the same time as your portfolio is reviewed or later.

Degree and HND courses

If you are applying for honours degree courses, Foundation degree courses or HND courses, you normally do so using the UCAS system.

Almost all applications are made online using the UCAS Hub. Further details can be found on the UCAS website and in the book *How to Complete Your UCAS Application* (see Chapter 12), but a brief overview of the process is given here.

The deadline for UCAS undergraduate applications is 13 January at 6 pm (courses at Oxford and Cambridge have an earlier deadline of 15 October at 6 pm). In total, you can choose five university courses.

Further details are available on the UCAS website, or from the institutions themselves.

The personal statement

Applications through UCAS will require a personal statement. You need to plan this very carefully, as it will significantly affect your chances of gaining an interview or being offered a place.

The personal statement is divided into three questions which provide students with scaffolding and structure. The three questions are:

- Why do you want to study this course or subject?
- How have your qualifications and studies helped you to prepare for this course or subject?
- What else have you done to prepare outside of education, and why are these experiences useful?

Further information can be found at: www.ucas.com/about-us/news-and-insights/reforming-admissions.

Many application forms give you enough space to write 300–500 words in support of your application, and the UCAS online application form gives you 4,000 characters. They generally specify the information that they are looking for. For example, the application webpage for the Central Saint Martins Foundation course suggests you describe why you have selected the course, your current creative practice and how the course will help you to achieve your future plans. Then it asks you to state any relevant education and experience you have. As you have a limited word count, your statement needs to be planned carefully. A good response might include a list of your particular interests, but you must make sure that they are relevant to the course you are applying for – there is no point in writing too much about your love of textiles if you are applying for a Foundation course that specialises in photography and media.

You should try to cover the following:

- What are your reasons for choosing the course?
- Why did you select the institution that you've chosen?
- What is your current creative practice and how will this course help you achieve your future plans?
- What artists and styles inspire you?
- What exhibitions have you seen?
- What areas of art do you enjoy? (e.g. fine art, graphics)
- How would you describe some of your own recent work?
- What are your career goals? How can this course help you achieve them?
- What relevant education and experience have you had? (This is especially important if you do not have any formal academic qualifications.)

> **TIP!**
>
> Attending open days or degree shows is important if you are to convince the admissions tutors that you are serious about your application. More information about open days is given in Chapters 2 and 3.

The best way to demonstrate your enthusiasm for art is to talk about your own work. This also gives the admissions staff an idea of your interests in a specific, rather than general, way. It is a good idea to try to include a contemporary artist, as you want to show the selectors that your interest in art is a developing one and that you are keen to be part of the current art scene rather than immersing yourself wholly in the past.

> **Personal statement 1 – Foundation course**
>
> ***Why do you want to study this course or subject?***
>
> I am applying for your art Foundation course because I want to broaden and refine my creative practice through experimentation, collaboration and exposure to a wide range of disciplines. I am excited by the opportunity to develop new skills, challenge my ideas and learn from tutors and fellow students.

My work often sits at the intersection of science and art, an area that continually inspires me to look closer and reinterpret the unseen. I was awarded the Science and Art Sixth Form Scholarship, which encouraged me to explore creative projects informed by scientific processes. I am particularly fascinated by microbiology; the hidden patterns, textures, and structures that exist beyond the naked eye, and much of my current work grows from this fascination. The Foundation course appeals to me because of its emphasis on experimentation and interdisciplinary practice, which aligns perfectly with my approach to artmaking and my desire to explore the connections between observation, material and concept.

How have your qualifications and studies helped you to prepare for this course or subject?

In my current project, I am experimenting with photographs I took through a microscope lens, exploring how these images can be developed into more abstract visual outcomes. One of these photographs was highly commended in the Royal Academy Youth Summer Exhibition and is displayed on their website. This recognition gave me confidence in my ideas and encouraged me to push my work further.

My exploration of microscopic imagery naturally led me to etching, a process that echoes the intricate structures of the cells I study. I was particularly inspired by Norman Ackroyd's misty, atmospheric prints, which influenced both the tone and texture of my A level coursework. My AS final piece was entered into the UpStArt competition, where it reached the final round, was exhibited at the Strand Gallery, and later auctioned for charity. These experiences taught me how to develop an idea from research through to public exhibition and helped me understand the value of reflection and refinement in creative work.

I have also developed an interest in textiles. This year, I am working as an apprentice for a Japanese designer alongside my A level studies. Through this experience, I have learned to respect materials and respond to their qualities: to understand a fabric's grain, explore its strength and accept its unpredictability. Balancing this apprenticeship with schoolwork has taught me time management and adaptability, while also deepening my appreciation for process, craftsmanship and collaboration.

What else have you done to prepare outside of education, and why are these experiences useful?

Through my studies and experiences, I have developed a curiosity-driven approach to making art, one that values experimentation, observation and interdisciplinary thinking. I am drawn to creative environments that encourage dialogue, where ideas can evolve through both making and critique.

Your Foundation course offers the perfect opportunity to experiment with new media before specialising, particularly within fashion and textile design, which I am eager to explore further. I look forward to learning from peers who bring diverse perspectives and approaches, as collaboration often sparks my most innovative ideas.

Beyond my studies, I am motivated, organised and open-minded. My background in both science and art has shaped me into a reflective, analytical thinker who enjoys problem-solving through making. I hope to continue developing as an artist and designer, eventually pursuing a creative career that combines scientific observation with visual storytelling. The Foundation course would provide the ideal environment to explore these interests and define the next stage of my creative journey.

Personal statement 2 – Foundation course

Why do you want to study this course or subject?

When reflecting on Frida Kahlo's 'What Water Gave Me', I am struck by how she used art as a means of self-expression and personal storytelling. Her work made me think about what would appear in my own bathtub; the imagery, experiences and influences that have shaped who I am as an artist. For me, art has always been a way to understand both myself and the world around me, combining personal experience with wider cultural and historical contexts.

Your Foundation Diploma in Art and Design at Manchester appeals to me because it will allow me to explore a wide range of disciplines before choosing a specialism, developing both my practical skills and conceptual understanding. I am eager to experiment with different materials and approaches, and to work within a community that values curiosity and collaboration.

I am drawn to the Foundation Diploma at Manchester because it offers the freedom to experiment with techniques and concepts, and to develop work that is both expressive and informed. I am excited by the city's creative energy and by its personal connection to my family roots. Ultimately, I hope to continue exploring how art can communicate identity, experience and story, just as Frida Kahlo did, through a language that is entirely my own.

How have your qualifications and studies helped you to prepare for this course or subject?

Sitting on the rim of my bathtub is me, holding a camera. I recently completed work experience as a production assistant for Gilly Booth at Hijack Films, working on a documentary about Eduardo Paolozzi. I took production stills during interviews and photographed Paolozzi's artworks held in private collections. This gave me valuable insight into the relationship between film and fine art, and how visual storytelling operates across different media.

Studying A level photography has allowed me to develop this interest further, combining image-making with research and critical reflection. Photography has become another language for me, a way to document and reimagine reality.

Growing up surrounded by culture, frequent visits to art galleries and the theatre encouraged me not only to appreciate art but to understand the craft, thought and context behind it. Studying History of Art has deepened this understanding, giving me insight into technique, meaning and intention, while also helping me to define my own creative voice.

What else have you done to prepare outside of education, and why are these experiences useful?

Gently floating in my bathtub would be the houseboat where I grew up, a symbol of creativity and individuality. My Dutch father, Mancunian mother, and four sisters each express their passions through literature, drama, politics, sport, dance and art. As the houseboat drifts across the water, it moves towards a vibrant and colourful landscape; Spain, where I am dancing flamenco with my sisters. I have trained in flamenco for ten years, and it mirrors how I approach art: both are forms of release and self-expression, requiring rhythm, discipline and emotion.

Close to my feet in the bathtub sits the Tate Modern, a place that has played a defining role in my creative journey. It was there that my passion for artists such as Madame Yevonde, Matisse and Frida Kahlo first developed. I was selected by the Tate to join their Raw Canvas team, later becoming a staff member involved in developing the Youth Programme. My role has included organising events, conducting research trips to Paris and New York, and exploring how galleries engage young audiences. This experience has taught me about curation, communication and accessibility, as well as the importance of collaboration and encouraging others to engage with art from different perspectives.

Personal statement 3 - Foundation course application

Why do you want to study this course or subject?

My love for fashion and art began with admiration for those who use their creative platform as a form of activism; people who take something as everyday as the fibres we wear and transform it into a statement of resistance. I was fascinated by how designers like Jean Paul Gaultier, who challenged gender norms by putting men in skirts, and artists such as Renate Bertlmann, who used garments and accessories as avant-garde feminist symbols, redefined what fashion could mean. Their work taught me that creativity can challenge expectations and become a powerful form of social commentary.

This admiration evolved into a personal motivation to create work that not only looks beautiful but carries meaning. I am drawn to designers such as Hussein Chalayan, whose collection *Before Minus Now* (AW00) transforms unambiguous objects into wearable ideas, redefining how fashion communicates with the world around it. I see fashion as a language, one capable of expressing complex ideas about culture, gender and identity. The Foundation Diploma in Art and Design, with its emphasis on experimentation and conceptual development, is the ideal next step for me to explore how visual and material choices can articulate these ideas through textiles and fashion.

How have your qualifications and studies helped you to prepare for this course or subject?

As I have developed my practice in textiles and fashion, I've discovered a passion for process, for creating pieces that are tactile, experimental and layered with meaning. My approach is hands-on and exploratory: I love using embroidery and fabric manipulation techniques such as trapunto, cross-shirring and smocking, combining them in unexpected ways to create abstract outcomes.

What excites me most is how these experiments often take on a life of their own. The process of transforming simple materials into something expressive and surprising continually reminds me that creativity involves both control and spontaneity. Through my coursework, I've learned to balance technique with concept, ensuring that each piece not only demonstrates skill but also communicates emotion and intent.

I am inspired by designers such as Rei Kawakubo and Yohji Yamamoto, who use the human form as a canvas for reinvention. Their work challenges traditional ideas of beauty by reconstructing the silhouette rather than conforming to it. I aspire to take a similar approach, using fabric, structure, and manipulation to question what is considered 'normal' and to push against the boundaries of conventional design.

5| How to Apply

> **What else have you done to prepare outside of education, and why are these experiences useful?**
>
> Alongside my studies, I completed an internship with the creative production agency Sylvia Farago Ltd, where I assisted with the production of editorials and campaigns for clients including Topshop, Adidas, Stüssy and Vogue. Working within a professional studio exposed me to the fast-paced nature of the fashion industry and gave me insight into the collaborative processes behind successful creative projects. I learned how to problem-solve, adapt quickly and communicate ideas effectively, all skills that I will bring to my Foundation studies.
>
> Being surrounded by leading figures in fashion refined my aesthetic and deepened my understanding of how the industry operates beyond design. It opened my eyes to the diverse roles within the creative world, from production and styling to art direction. Through this experience, I discovered that my path lies in fashion design and styling, where I can merge my technical understanding of garments with a conceptual and expressive approach.
>
> The Foundation Diploma will allow me to strengthen my knowledge of fabric, form and construction, while also developing my ability to translate ideas into three-dimensional garments that communicate mood, identity, and message. I am eager to continue exploring how fashion can be both a personal and political act, a medium through which creativity becomes a voice for change.

Notice that the personal statements include details of artists that the applicants are interested in. Never drop in the names of artists or galleries/exhibitions that you have visited without giving some indication of why they are important to you. The point of the personal statement is to demonstrate that you not only enjoy art in a practical sense, but also think about it.

> **WARNING!**
>
> Do not put things into the personal statement simply to impress the selectors. If you do get to the interview stage, you may be asked to talk about one or more of the artists or exhibitions that you have mentioned, and the surest way to be rejected is to be caught out. You might be tempted to get external help in writing the personal statement, and of course it is a good idea to get advice and feedback from teachers, your parents and anyone else who can help. You may be aware of the many websites that offer to prepare the personal statement for you, for a fee. UCAS uses anti-plagiarism software to check each statement, and you may have your application cancelled if it appears that the work is not your own.

> Similarly, it may be tempting to use Artificial Intelligence (AI) software to write your personal statement for you, but UCAS will be able to use software that can detect if a passage is written by AI. Furthermore, while these methods may help to create a statement that looks well written, it will not have the same meaningful content about you, and university admissions teams will not be impressed by a well-written statement that says nothing specific.

Another key element in the personal statement should be something to lead the reader to ask you a specific question at interview for which you have prepared an outstanding answer. In the UCAS application examples above, the applicants describe, briefly, their own work, but cannot give much detail. They can be reasonably confident that, if invited to interview, they will be asked more about these pieces of work, and so they can prepare for this part of the interview in advance.

Individuality

The sample personal statements shown above are well structured and demonstrate the applicants' interest in art and what they have done to find out more. But remember that if you are applying to art schools, you are intent on following a course that requires creativity and an ability to convey what is inside your head into things that other people will relate to or want to use. So do not be afraid to be, as someone involved in admissions at one art school puts it, 'quirky' in what you put in your personal statement. If you have interesting ideas or interesting ways of demonstrating your passion for art or design, by all means use them. This could take the form of an anecdote, a quotation, an event or piece of art that inspired you, a poem, a dialogue ... anything that helps you to show your creative side and where your ideas come from.

What to avoid

The personal statement is just that – a statement that reflects your interests and influences. There are some things to avoid at all costs.

- You must avoid using very general statements that say nothing about you. 'I have always been interested in art, and get great enjoyment from my work,' without an explanation or description of specific areas of interest or pieces of work, will not give the selectors anything to go on.
- Writing 'I would like to come to your college because of the facilities' is too general: say which facilities and why they attract you. Bring in your own areas of interest if possible.
- Never make judgements about artists, their work or exhibitions without backing them up: 'I went to see the John Craxton exhibition at the Dorset County Museum and I liked it' is not going to impress anyone. The admissions tutors would be more won over, however,

if you added 'because it was fascinating to see how his paintings and prints were influenced by lesser-known artists who lived there. Craxton had cousins who lived locally and so he was exposed to a variety of painters whose work was based around representing the landscapes around them. This inspired me to look at other British artists who also worked in the South West, including John Piper.'

Scottish art schools and colleges

As already mentioned in Chapter 2, the system in Scotland is slightly different: most degree courses are four years in length and incorporate the equivalent of a Foundation course. In some cases, students can enter the second year directly if they have undertaken a suitable Foundation or portfolio preparation course. For details, you should contact the institutions directly. In both cases, application is made through UCAS.

Non-standard applications

Not everyone who applies for Foundation courses is an A level (or equivalent) student. Similarly, some people apply for degree courses without having studied on a Foundation course. The main categories of 'non-standard' applicants are mature students (for further and higher education purposes, anyone over the age of 21) and overseas students. If you fall into one of these categories, you should make direct contact with the colleges that interest you to discuss your situation. Many applicants who are not classed as 'mature' or 'international' students but who nevertheless do not have the 'standard' qualifications for entry gain places on art courses every year. It may be because they took A levels in, for example, science subjects; or they left school at 16 and went to work. If you are in this situation, the first port of call will be the art schools, which will be able to give you advice about their particular requirements. This might involve some short courses, evening classes, a 'pre-Foundation' course (see 'Alternative routes' in Chapter 6) or other relevant preparation.

The colleges' websites and prospectuses will also contain sections aimed at you. It is important to be aware that, for all applicants, in addition to your personal qualities, the portfolio is the most important element in the application. Without a promising portfolio, you will not be offered a place. Make sure that you read Chapter 7, which offers detailed advice on this.

Mature students

You may already have either a portfolio of work that you undertook when you were at school (in which case, it will probably need updating), or perhaps a collection of pieces that you have been working on recently. It is often helpful to get guidance from art teachers, and for this reason many mature students will take evening classes, portfolio classes or Access courses before applying. (Sometimes this is best done at the college to which you intend to apply.)

Application to postgraduate courses is covered in Chapter 11.

Preparation for your application

Make sure you stand out from the others.

- Visit galleries and exhibitions on a regular basis.
- Keep a notebook and a camera/smartphone with you at all times to record things that interest you.
- Try to get your work exhibited in school exhibitions, your local library, local cafes – anywhere where people will see your work.
- Try to arrange some relevant work experience – this could be in a gallery, a museum, an art studio or with a designer or an architect. Getting work experience in a creative field is not always easy, and you will need to use your contacts to find out what opportunities might be available and how best to approach them – use your friends, friends of friends, your friends' parents, your parents, your parents' friends, your teachers, your teachers' friends – anyone who can help!

'By being given the opportunity to study textiles at A level, I was able to have the chance of starting to explore the world of fashion from a textiles point of view. Fortunately, we were taught at a very mature level which has made it easier for me to transition from A levels straight to a BA in fashion design. By developing a close relationship with my tutors, I was not only able to enjoy myself but also produce outcomes that challenged my skills. By being set work for specific deadlines, it has helped me with the university workload and my time management. Through the help of my tutors, I was lucky enough to have the opportunity to intern for Julien MacDonald, which was an amazing experience.

'I am in a much larger creative environment now, where I am surrounded by so many talented individuals. I am so fortunate to have the opportunity to study here. Although the workload is considerably larger than A levels, I know that everything I am doing now is a step closer to my career in the industry. Studying fashion design at university is tough, there is a huge amount of not just work but also the immense amount of research that goes into being able to produce final outcomes that are backed up by evidence and interest.'

Holly R, BA Fashion Design, Ravensbourne Art College

6 | International students

Students from all over the world come to the UK to study on art or design courses. Many UK institutions are recognised internationally as being the best in the world. In 2024, over 3,800 overseas students gained places on art or design degree courses. Many of these students will have followed Foundation courses in the UK for a year. If you want to be a fashion designer, an architect or a product designer, or if you want to train to work in the creative sides of TV, film, IT or advertising, studying in the UK will give you the best possible preparation and qualifications.

Following Britain's withdrawal from the EU, European students (EU, EEA and Swiss) are now considered international students. They are no longer granted home fee status or eligible to receive loans from Student Finance, and will have to be granted a visa to study in the UK. Unless exempt (see below), European nationals will have to apply as international students.

Exemptions only apply to those with Irish citizenship or European nationals who have successfully applied to the EU settlement scheme. There are also some special categories applicable to circumstances, such as humanitarian protection and victims of abuse, that allow for home status equivalent eligibility.

In response to these changes, many institutions have introduced more scholarships and other financial schemes available to European students, so it is worth enquiring about your eligibility for these. The institution to which you are applying will normally be able to offer support and advice for European students regarding these rules.

The majority of unsuccessful international applicants fail not because they are not committed to or not suitable for their course, but simply because they are not fully aware of how to submit a successful application. Since you are reading this chapter, you have already increased your chances of success significantly!

NB: Students who are interested in architecture may already be aware that the regulations for architectural training in the UK mean that UK architecture qualifications will allow them to work anywhere in the world. A significant proportion of the most exciting and high-profile architectural projects around the world in recent years have had an input from architects trained in the UK.

Most of the information contained in this book applies to international students as well as to home students. However, some aspects of the application procedures are different, and if you are applying to study art or design at Foundation, degree or postgraduate level you should be aware of this. The main differences are listed below:

- application deadlines;
- portfolio submission and interview process;
- alternative routes;
- fees (details can be found in Chapter 10);
- English language requirements.

Application deadlines

You should read the information on application routes and deadlines contained elsewhere in this book. Information on the application deadlines will be given on the individual institutions' websites. In some cases, international students can apply for these courses later than home students, and the dates for interviews may also be later in the year.

Portfolio submissions and interviews

In order for you to be offered a place to study art or design at an art college or a university, someone from that institution will need to look at examples of your work.

Most institutions will ask that you submit an online portfolio, and you may be interviewed via an online video call, but some institutions will have in-person portfolio reviews and interviews. Some institutions may also have representatives in other countries that you can apply to instead of applying directly; this will allow you to have an in-person interview.

The University of the Arts London offers several online and in-person short courses, specific to a variety of subjects, that are tailored to portfolio preparation. The cost of these courses typically starts from £680. This is a good way to experience learning at an institution as well as increasing your chances of a successful application, so it is worth checking whether an institution you are interested in offers such a course.

Under some circumstances (e.g. if you are considered to be too young for direct entry onto a Foundation course, or if your English is not sufficiently good) you may be advised to spend a year on a pre-Foundation course at a recommended school or college in the UK before proceeding to the Foundation course (see 'Alternative routes').

Alternative routes

Most international students follow the same route as UK students to their degree or postgraduate art and design courses; that is, a one-year Foundation course followed by a three-year BA course and then, in some cases, an MA course. Some universities, such as Norwich University of the Arts (www.nua.ac.uk), run four-year degree programmes to ensure that international students are fully prepared. UAL offers a six-month, online, pre-degree course for international students. Completing this course will guarantee a place on undergraduate courses specialising in art, design and communication (excluding fashion, textiles and jewellery).

Pre-university art education varies considerably in content and delivery from country to country (for instance, in the balance between technical skills and original ideas), so some international students are not accepted directly onto Foundation courses. Others may have the potential to start a Foundation course, but they may be too young or may not reach the required standard of English. Students in this situation may be advised by universities or art schools to spend an extra year in the UK prior to the Foundation course.

A popular route is to spend a year in a UK school or college either following an art pre-Foundation course (an art and design-related course together with, if necessary, English classes) or studying on one-year accelerated A level courses. This route would be recommended by the university or art school at the interview or portfolio review stage. Many art schools will have partner institutions that can provide these courses.

An alternative route for those international students who are too young to go directly onto an Art Foundation course is to attend the International School of Creative Arts (ISCA), an independent boarding school near London, which opened in July 2009 in association with the University of the Arts London. The school provides pre-university training for British and overseas students to prepare them to enter a university course in the arts and related disciplines. In addition to two-year A level courses in a range of art and design subjects (with the option of adding academic subjects in combination with these), the school also offers a one-year portfolio programme, designed for those who possess the academic qualifications for university entrance but need to develop a portfolio. It also offers an online Foundation Diploma. Further information can be found on the school's website (www.isca.uk.com).

English language requirements

You should refer to the individual institutions for their requirements. To give you an idea of what level of English is required, the University of the Arts London asks:

- Foundation Diploma, pre-degree online: IELTS 5.0;
- Bachelor of Arts undergraduate: IELTS 6.0;
- Master of Arts: IELTS 6.5;
- Master of Research: IELTS 7.0.

Information on IELTS (International English Language Testing System), TOEFL test and other accepted English language qualifications can be found on the UK Council for International Student Affairs (UKCISA) website – details in Chapter 12.

Visas

For many international students, a visa is necessary to be able to study in the UK. The type of visa and the English language requirements necessary to obtain the visa vary from course to course and are liable to change periodically. The university and college websites will give details of what they ask for in terms of English and will also give guidance about visa issues.

Students from outside the UK will usually need a student visa (also referred to as the 'student route' of application) to study in the UK. You can apply online for a student visa on the gov.uk website or at one of the local visa application centres which are listed on the gov.uk website.

Nationals from the EU, EEA and Switzerland are considered 'low-risk applicants', and as such do not have to submit as much information as applicants from other regions when applying for a student visa. (Irish nationals and European nationals with settled status do not need a visa to study.)

To apply for a student visa, you:

- Must have an unconditional offer of a place on a course. Once you have been offered a place, your institution will send you a Confirmation of Acceptance for Studies (CAS) reference number. You must have a CAS reference number before making a visa application. If you have more than one offer, you must decide where you intend to study and use the CAS from that institution when you apply.
- Must prove your knowledge of the English language (reading, writing, speaking and understanding); there are some exemptions to this, including if you are from or have previously studied in certain countries considered as majority English-speaking countries or have studied at a school in the UK.

6| International Students

- Must show evidence of possessing sufficient finances to pay for one academic year's fees. You may also need to show you can afford living expenses when staying in the UK:
    - £1,529 per month (for up to nine months) for courses in London;
    - £1,171 per month (for up to nine months) for courses outside London.

A student visa application costs £524. You will also need to pay the immigration health surcharge of £776 for each year of the visa for which you are applying. The institution at which you are intending to study will be able to offer guidance on the visa application process. Further guidance can be found at the UK Council for International Student Affairs (UKCISA).

7 | Putting together a portfolio

For most students making the move into further or higher education, the offer of a place is normally made on the basis of past academic performance, personal statements and references, predicted grades for forthcoming examinations and, increasingly, an interview. With art school applicants, all of the above applies but with one very important addition: you will need to show your work in a portfolio. Above all, colleges want to know who you are, what you have done and, most importantly, what your potential is. Demonstrating these things is the function of the portfolio.

If you are interviewed alongside your portfolio submission (discussed in Chapter 8), you will deliver your portfolio, the college will look at it and in the interview, you will get the chance to talk about it and yourself, as well as to ask and answer questions.

For some, this may seem a daunting prospect. Most artists worry about showing their work to others. It is not surprising when you think about it. Having put our heart and soul into what we do, naturally we worry about negative judgements. Do not panic! Attending an interview with a portfolio of your work gives you a big advantage. Unlike your contemporaries who rarely get the chance to show what they can do except in exams, not only do you get to show what you are best at – being creative – but you also have plenty of time to prepare in advance, a good idea of what to expect, and all the people interviewing you will be artists themselves, so they will understand what you are doing.

What is a portfolio?

A portfolio is a folder containing examples of art and design work. Professional artists and designers need to take their portfolios to job interviews. You will show your portfolio to the admissions tutors of the courses to which you apply. Portfolios come in all shapes and sizes, and in many cases, you will be able to use the same one (normally A2 size) in which to display your work for both Foundation and degree applications (though obviously the contents will be different!).

There are some exceptions. For example, a student applying for a specialist degree course in photography might choose to use a portfolio specifically designed for that purpose. They are often smaller and are

7| Putting Together a Portfolio

sometimes referred to as 'books'. In fact, the term 'portfolio' can be used to describe any collection of works for presentation even if they are not actually displayed exclusively in a folder. Some institutions or courses may require the portfolio to be submitted online.

Which portfolio should you buy?

At this stage, do not buy one at all. Wait until you have read the whole of this book, have had a chance to think things over and, most importantly, have some idea of what you are going to put in it. As a guide, buy the best one that you can afford, as it will protect your work better and be a saving in the long term. Look at the quality of the zip if it has one and check that the ring binder works well. Is the handle strong and comfortable? When thinking about sizes, consider how big your work is. On the other hand, do not bite off more than you can chew. If you cannot carry it, it is too big! Above all, though, remember that it is the quality of your work that counts and not the quality of the thing that you carry it in.

Getting your work together

The following guidelines apply to portfolios for both Foundation and degree course applications. Read them carefully: they describe the qualities that you should look for in your work and will help you make decisions about which pieces to select. Later in this chapter, there are also sections giving guidance on the requirements for each type of portfolio. Make sure you read the contributions made by course tutors.

The first step in putting together your portfolio is to gather together all of your work. When you do this, it might be tempting to say 'I won't need that' or 'That's no good', but at this stage, just concentrate on getting all of your work in one place so you can see what you have got: finished pieces, unfinished pieces, sketchbooks, models, notebooks, written work, old work, new work – get everything! This is important because not only will you find things that have been tucked away that are actually very good, but also, as you look through your work, you will begin to see relationships emerging between new and old pieces. A small sketch that at first may seem rather unimpressive might have inspired a later, much more accomplished piece. The ability to make judgements and to evaluate what you have done, to recognise a good idea and to develop it further, is an important part of the creative process. Admissions tutors will be assessing to what extent you are able to do these things – they want to see the process, not just the finished work.

It may help you to organise your work into categories. The following list will provide you with a starting point:

- contextual studies/written work;
- drawings from observation;
- drawings of invention;
- finished pieces;
- life drawings;
- models and maquettes;
- sketchbooks/journals;
- sketches and studies;
- works in progress.

The importance of drawing

Albert Einstein used the formula $E = mc^2$ to express his famous theory of relativity. Scientists use mathematics to express and explore their understanding of the world and how it works. Artists and designers do this with drawing.

Drawing could usefully be described as the act of making marks to convey meaning. Artists and designers use drawing to record observations, work out ideas, pass on information, express feelings and emotions and resolve practical problems. Drawings are often used to help us visualise how things fit together. For example, scale drawing can be used to work out whether all the units of a kitchen will fit into the space available. Diagrams and flowcharts can be used to demonstrate how ideas and principles relate to each other. Drawings come in all shapes and sizes and are made with a variety of different purposes in mind. Examples of types of drawing include:

- life drawings;
- observational drawings, such as those done from a still life or made in the field (e.g. architectural details);
- plans and designs;
- sketches and drafts.

Whichever course you apply to, the admissions tutors will want to see your drawings in one form or another because they are evidence of your visual intelligence and thought process. Your drawings demonstrate that you can perceive, understand, invent and communicate visually. These abilities are at the core of successful art making.

Sketchbooks

Sketchbooks fulfil many purposes. They are a place in which artists and designers begin the creative process. They are also a place in which to store cuttings, postcards and virtually any other articles that will fit. They are a place in which you can put your ideas, thoughts and feelings down on paper. Typically, interesting sketchbooks contain visualisations of many types, made by you for a variety of reasons.

These images might take the form of carefully studied observational drawings or quick sketches or doodles. In a sketchbook, you will refer back to previous ideas and make relationships between the images on one page and those on another. Perhaps you have spent some time experimenting with different ways of making marks. You will be familiar with many of the effects that you can get with a pencil, but what kind of drawings could you make with a nail? A sketchbook or journal is the place where you might try something like this. Maybe you have been using your sketchbook to work out the volume of a space so you can calculate how much concrete you would need to fill it. Why would you want to know? At this stage, you are probably not completely sure, and you do not need to be.

The sketchbook is a place where you can try things out even if they seem crazy; it will reveal the extent of your curiosity. In this sense, sketchbooks can be highly personal and frequently become much cherished. They also provide evidence of your creative development because they are time-based.

With very few exceptions, course admissions tutors will want to see your sketchbook work.

Project work

Project pieces might be two- or three-dimensional or time-based (such as video) and may use a variety of media. Normally they will have been completed on your current course of study and will show to what extent you have taken advantage of the training and support you have been given.

The ability to undertake and complete a project, whether it is self-determined or in response to a set brief, is one of the qualities that prospective art schools and colleges look for. Work developed over an extended period – formed by experimentation, contemplation, reflection and risk-taking – says a great deal about its creator.

- Are you willing to stick with something to the end?
- Will you test a theory to the point of destruction?
- Can you keep an open mind?

A project piece will demonstrate your imagination, invention and skill and give evidence of your willingness to condense your theories and commit to a final outcome. If it has been made as part of a group project, it will also show your ability to work with others. It can also be very helpful to include some work in progress in your portfolio. Unfinished pieces can have a freshness and ambiguity that often stimulates conversation.

Overly prepared portfolios in which everything is polished to perfection may come across as stifled and dishonest, and show little of your process; including an unfinished piece or two will help to avoid this problem.

Personal work

Most artists and designers have a strong desire to be creative. Whether they are extrovert or introvert by nature, creative people have a need to express themselves. Inevitably, this does not stop when you leave the classroom or studio. Personal work may take a variety of forms, but its essential qualities are that you did it because you wanted to; it contains your own opinions, thoughts and feelings; and it was made to fulfil your needs. Maybe you feel strongly about something and want to make a point or perhaps you are in a band, have recorded a demo and need a CD cover. In both cases, you would naturally have a need to create. Personal work says a lot about who you are and demonstrates your passion and commitment.

Contextual studies/written work

Written work is often overlooked at interview but should be included if possible. At degree level, it will be a requirement to complete some form of contextual study, and on a Foundation course, you can expect to be fully engaged in critical thinking (although you probably will not be required to produce an extended written piece). Reflecting on the work of others and responding to its qualities are fundamental parts of the creative process. This work will give you the chance to demonstrate your ability to explore ideas and concepts and learn from the work of others and, in many cases, will show how you are able to make choices about typefaces, justifying text and formatting illustrations.

Matching your portfolio to the course specification

Make sure that you read the course's portfolio specification thoroughly. Talk things through to make sure that you are clear about what is required. Each course will have its own requirements. For example, many courses ask you to limit your portfolio to a particular number of pieces. Whatever the requirements are, respect them; they will be there for a reason and are your best guide to what to include. In many cases, it will be necessary for you to adapt your portfolio for each course to which you apply. Make sure that you give yourself time to do this.

Special considerations

It may not be possible to take all of your work to the interview; perhaps it is too big or too fragile. For practical reasons, art schools and colleges inevitably have to put some restrictions on what can be accepted. If this is the case, in most instances it is perfectly acceptable to take photographs, but do check with the admissions tutors first. Original work is preferable if possible, and if you do take photographs, make sure that they are good ones.

> **TIP!**
>
> Label your portfolio – make sure that you clearly identify your work. You do not want there to be any confusion about who did it, and you want to make sure that you will get it back. This is particularly important if you have to submit your portfolio in advance of the interview – do put your name and address in an obvious place.

Digital portfolios

Many institutions accept or even encourage you to submit your portfolio digitally. This could be in one of a number of formats:

- uploading images of your work to a web-based site such as Flickr or YouTube;
- submitting your work as a PDF portfolio;
- creating your own website or blog in which to showcase your work.

Your chosen institution will give you advice on the number of pieces, the type of work it wants to see, technical information on the format it wants the work in and how to upload it or send it.

> **TIP!**
>
> Ensure that you use digital file sizes that are neither too large (in case they cannot be attached to an email or downloaded easily) nor too small so that the quality of the image is not sufficient for a selector to assess your work.
>
> If you are photographing your paintings, drawings or 3D pieces, use a good-quality camera and ensure the lighting is good. Avoid shadows, reflections, camera glare or distracting backgrounds.
>
> Make sure that everything is labelled clearly: your name, any titles of the works, when they were made and any other information you feel is important. This might include materials you used, techniques or influences.

Your portfolio

Robert Green, previously Manager of International Student Support at the University of the Arts London, gives advice about portfolios:

'The majority of our courses at the University of the Arts London are studio/practice-focused, and as such, entry is generally based on portfolio assessment and interview. Therefore, careful preparation and selection of the portfolio is an essential preliminary to the interview.

'The portfolio is a visual diary. It is the documentation of the individual's journey, both perceptually and conceptually, over a period of time. In essence, the portfolio should be comprehensive, demonstrating a breadth and depth of inquiry, curiosity and genuine investigation. Solid practical skills and experience of working with a variety of media and techniques are, in addition, of equal importance.

'The portfolio should include work done in school or college and at home. The range of approaches and the materials used should show that the applicant has made the most of the opportunities around them, in terms both of what they are being taught and the art room or studio facilities that are available. We particularly look for evidence that an applicant has been prepared to develop some ideas further on their own initiative and in their own time.

'Time and care are needed in selecting the portfolio, and systematic decisions about what to include and how to organise and present the work should be made. Obvious repetition should be avoided, as should over-selection. A limited number of relevant works in progress may be included because, first and foremost, we are looking for potential.

'Ideally, a portfolio should consist of between 25 and 50 pieces of recent work, completed over a two-year period. This collection of work should show evidence of a broad-based creativity and include sketchbooks, visual research books, idea sheets and any experiments or explorations in three dimensions. The portfolio should demonstrate, through project and thematically based work, evidence of individual creativity and the development of ideas. Generally, it is important that work reflects and demonstrates creative thinking and a personal commitment to a particular project.

'In the early stages of all our courses, we concentrate on combining technical workshops with set projects. As courses progress, assignments generally become more wide-ranging and contextually based. All practical work is undertaken within a framework of individual and group tutorials as well as studio criticism sessions, where all students are encouraged to offer constructive critical opinions and advice to each other. Critical exchange and dialogue is central to our teaching approach.

'Therefore, at interview, all applicants are expected to discuss and evaluate the development and context of their work so as to demonstrate broad understanding and an ability to think critically.

7| Putting Together a Portfolio

> 'A portfolio is not a mere supplement to an interview, but is the main factor in assessing a student's future potential. Thus the portfolio is even more essential to students who are unable to be interviewed.
>
> 'You could present your portfolio in the form of colour photographs or colour photocopies. However, most likely, you will be asked to digitise your folder and upload it to a chosen site. You should send between 25 and 50 pieces of work.
>
> 'The University of the Arts London has representatives in a number of countries across the world. Our representatives can assist with all aspects of the application procedure, offer information about programmes and courses and assist with immigration matters.
>
> 'When our senior academics make their next scheduled visit, a local representative can arrange for applicants to have an interview or an advice session with an academic. Our contact details and an overseas schedule can be found on our website.'

Enrolling on short courses

Short courses can be a valuable source of extra tuition. They give you a taster of what being at art school is like and can be a lot of fun. For mature applicants, they provide the opportunity to work with teachers and become reacquainted with a teaching environment. If you do not have access to a life model, for example, consider taking life-drawing classes. Courses could be theoretical in nature and could cross over into other disciplines that are new to you, for example, animation. Not only will this help to build up your portfolio, but it will also be an excellent demonstration of your commitment.

Taking a short course at a university you are considering attending is a good way of expressing your interest, and you may even meet and build a relationship with the admissions tutors. Some institutions, such as the University of the Arts London, offer portfolio preparation short courses.

Portfolio reviews

Many schools and colleges offer portfolio review sessions, sometimes leading up to mock interviews. Certainly, your teacher or tutor will offer you advice and support. Remember, you are not always the best judge of what to put in and what to leave out of your portfolio. You are going to need a second opinion, and taking the advice of an experienced teacher will help enormously.

Freak-outs

Most artists feel overwhelmed from time to time – it often goes with the territory for those of us who are willing to test things to the limit. The process of putting together a portfolio can feel stressful at the best of times, and if you leave everything to the last minute, it will be even worse. You also need to make sure you leave time to think about what you are going to say at interview.

When a group of A level students applying to art school were asked 'If you could give a fellow art school applicant one piece of advice on how to put together a portfolio, what would it be?', their unanimous response – which they all shouted out – was 'Start early!' Setting manageable weekly deadlines and keeping an honest record of what you have and have not done will help enormously. Set specific goals such as 'I need more life drawing'. Not convinced? Read on.

> 'When putting together my portfolio, I wanted everything to be perfect, for every piece to look like something you might find in a gallery. However, after researching, reading and speaking with teachers, I realised that what universities really look for in a creative degree application is passion and curiosity. Show that alongside your technical skills, you're exploring new ideas and trying things that feel unique to you. And if a piece didn't turn out exactly as you hoped, tell them! Let them see your thought process as well as the final result. They're not just accepting your work, they're accepting you as an artist.'
>
> *Grace*

> 'The other students seemed so confident, so cool and were carrying so much work. I felt very intimidated. But the interview itself was much less stressful than I had thought. The interviewer asked me to choose one piece from my portfolio and explain its story – where I got the idea (from an exhibition I had been to), what preliminary work I did (I showed him some sketches and colour swatches in my notebook) and how I would develop the idea (I hadn't thought about this but talked a bit about incorporating some collage into it next time). He smiled and encouraged me all the time. And I was offered a place!'
>
> *Pat*

> 'I had two interviews for Foundation courses, at UAL and Kingston. The thing that they had in common was that the atmosphere was very relaxed in both interviews, more like a chat about my likes and future plans. The interviewers seemed interested in my portfolio work and allowed me to talk about the pieces I liked best, prompting

me with questions about ideas for future development of the pieces, or where I got the ideas from. The difference was that for one of the interviews, the university had run a workshop at my college a month before, on how to prepare for their interviews, so I not only knew what to expect but also had met my interviewer before. So I went in feeling confident. At the other interview, I had three people in the room asking me questions, so I was much more nervous. My advice for students applying is to find out as much as you can about the interview process in advance by talking to current students – ask your school for the names of previous students who have gone to the university.'

Charlotte

'To be honest, I really enjoyed the portfolio preparation process for my Foundation course. I was quite nervous the day before the interview, but practising and becoming more confident in talking about my work definitely helped. It was important to stay focused and try to remain calm. Going through my portfolio and double-checking that everything is in order was a good way to occupy myself and ensure I was prepared before my interview.'

Julia

'I hadn't been given much advice from my previous school about applying for art courses, and didn't realise that I needed to do Foundation. I just assumed that I would apply for the fashion degree I wanted to follow. My portfolio was full of fashion sketches but not much else. My UCAS applications were rejected without interview but one college did contact me and asked me to come to a Foundation interview. They were very nice but didn't offer me a place because my portfolio "showed no real variety or evidence of research". They advised me to take another year of A level and to do textiles and photography in a year and also get help on my portfolio. I was annoyed at first, but in fact, the extra year taught me so much about finding sources of ideas and developing them into something personal. I got offers from all of my chosen Foundation courses, and ended up here at UAL. My advice – research courses and their requirements.'

Billy

'Make sure you get someone to help you to practise before the real interview. Not to rehearse as if you were in a play, but by asking you questions about your work, ideas, future plans. I was lucky because my school organised practice interviews and portfolio crit sessions but I met some people at the interview who were very, very nervous because they had no idea what to expect.'

Libby

Foundation course portfolios

Your Foundation course portfolio should contain as wide a variety of work as possible. You may think that you are heading for a career in fashion design, but you are applying for a diagnostic course that aims to confirm that choice for you or point you in another direction. Tutors want to see potential in all sorts of areas, so include:

- colour work made in a variety of media;
- contextual studies or written work;
- drawings and paintings made from observation and imagination, using a variety of media;
- examples of design work and model-making;
- life drawings;
- multimedia work such as video;
- photography;
- photographs of three-dimensional work if it is not possible to transport it;
- printmaking;
- project work made on your current course and for yourself;
- sketchbooks.

Don't worry if you cannot include all of these; very few students are able to. Remember that admissions tutors will primarily be looking for potential and motivation.

What admissions tutors look for in a portfolio

Natalie Wyle and Is Bealey are Course Leaders for the Foundation Diploma in Art, Design and Media Practice at Kingston School of Art.

'The questions we get asked the most are: "What should I put in my portfolio?" or "What's the best thing to include in my portfolio?". While probably frustrating, our answer is always, well that depends on you! On Foundation at Kingston School of Art, we champion the sharing of ideas, experiences and outlooks. We're not looking for one type of applicant, but many. We believe that makes for a rich and meaningful studio environment.

'Applications to Foundation include a portfolio where we ask you to include:

5 photos of final outcomes: final outcomes are pieces of work you feel are resolved. These may be flat work, paintings, sculpture, installation, illustration, animation, film, garments, products, the list goes on.

15 photos of your working process: your working process should document how you come up with ideas, research into relevant subject matter or themes, your experimentation, things that might have gone wrong, surprising successes! You may have sketchbook pages, design development, process pages.

10 photos of "Draw This!" task: for the Draw This task we'd like you to create a series of **10 observational drawings in response to one of the ideas below.** Pick something that excites you and consider the drawing tools and materials you might use as well as the size and scale of the surface you may draw on.

- **Visit a place you haven't been before** and record what you find there through drawing. This should be somewhere accessible to you but could be a museum, park, building, event, gallery, public space and so on.
- **Watch a film/documentary you haven't seen before** and record the scenes, framing and narrative through drawing. This is a chance to explore a genre or subject of filmmaking or documentary you might not be as familiar with. Websites like the BFI / BBC Archive have a large collection of free content.
- **Record a journey you haven't done before** and document it through drawing. This might be a walk, bus or train journey, a cycle ... consider the places you may pass through, how a landscape might change where you start and where you end up. The length of the journey is up to you; we're interested in how you record it.

10 photos of "Things I Like": this could be 10 things that inspire you, things you collect, things you find hilarious ... think about how this can be as specific to you and your interests as possible. These do not have to relate to art and design.

'We've carefully chosen this selection of things as it gives you the opportunity to share with us the subject matter that's informing your ideas, the things you want to celebrate or perhaps challenge, your experiments, successes and the things that haven't gone to plan but which you've learnt from.

'Most importantly, we want to get a sense of what motivates you. We are, of course, interested in the work you're creating now, but are equally interested in your ambitions for what you want to do next and why. We're not looking for polish but potential.'

Specialist course portfolios

While this portfolio should contain a range of work demonstrating your all-round ability, you will obviously need to demonstrate a commitment to a particular area of study and show a level of skill and ability in that field. However, admissions tutors will be realistic about the extent to which you will have been able to develop your skills and will very much be looking for potential and motivation. Items to include are:

- colour work made in a variety of media;
- contextual studies or written work;

- drawings made from observation and imagination, using a variety of media;
- life drawings;
- personal work in your specialisation made for yourself;
- photography;
- photographs of three-dimensional work as required, if it is not possible to transport it;
- project work in your specialised area of study made on your current course;
- sketchbooks.

With respect to your specialist project work, use the following examples as a starting point for ideas on what to include. As a rule, your portfolio should contain a sustained project made within your proposed area of study. Contact the course admissions tutors if you are unsure about what to put in.

Fashion

Drawings, sketches and collages showing design development; final designs; toiles; photographs or actual examples of garments you have made; a collection of information on particular designers, fashion manufacturers or shops; a design project worked on to a brief; evidence that you read fashion magazines and follow developments on the catwalk.

Film, TV and animation

A short film that you may have made as part of a course project; scripts; storyboards; a subject-dedicated sketchbook; drawings; photography; evidence that you regularly watch films and read reviews.

Fine art

Paintings and/or sculptures, photographs, textiles and pieces of work produced to a negotiated brief; original pieces, produced entirely from your own ideas; evidence that you read art magazines and visit exhibitions.

Graphic design

Lettering; samples of freehand drawing; examples of work showing page layout; projects relating to advertising, publicity or packaging; typography; work completed to a brief, such as a complete publicity campaign for a product; digitally manipulated images; evidence that you read design magazines and visit exhibitions.

Illustration

Work done from direct observation; work related to a design and technology project (if applying for technical or scientific illustration courses); work done to a brief – for example, a piece done to illustrate pages of a particular book, with sample text and notes explaining how you set out to emphasise particular aspects; evidence that you read appropriate literature and visit exhibitions.

Product design

Drawings, diagrams, computer-aided designs; working notes showing that you understand the workshop processes necessary to manufacture the product; preliminary sketches; photographs of the finished article; evidence that you read design magazines and visit exhibitions.

Guidance on portfolio preparation for specialist courses

> 'Interviews are an opportunity for you to demonstrate your commitment and self-motivation to a chosen area of study, and to discuss aspects of your chosen course and ask any questions that you may have. You will be expected to display and discuss your portfolio. Portfolios should contain examples of work (both finished and in progress) that showcase your particular interests – not only course or school work, but also any independent work, including, for example, sketchbooks and any other evidence of your ideas, your interests and passion for your chosen area of study.
>
> 'The form of portfolio work desired would vary according to the area of study. For example, the BA (Hons) in Costume course would require extensive evidence of figurative drawing whereas the BA (Hons) in Model-making would require that you show items that you have made, whether in pottery, wood or fabric. The common requirement across the board of courses is that you show evidence of your commitment to your area of study and an ability to visually express your ideas and concepts and show the creative development of your artwork from start to finish. The creative process is an important feature rather than the outcome. Passion for your chosen area of study is also essential as well as the ability to demonstrate and show your potential within a variety of artwork pieces.'
>
> Astrid MacKellar, Arts University Bournemouth

The skills your portfolio should demonstrate

- **Drawing**: evidence of life drawing can be useful because it demonstrates such a particular discipline, but any drawing that shows you can observe and interpret the world around you is

important. Drawings can be any scale and in any medium, but a diversity of approaches shows exploration and a keenness to experiment.
- **Problem-solving**: your ability to solve visual problems can be demonstrated through design sheets or sketchbooks, but should show in detail how you would deal with design briefs or your own (if more fine art-based) issues or ideas. If anything, these are the most revealing parts of the interview, and for many staff, they are more important than seeing finished pieces.
- **Diversity**: a diversity of work and a willingness to experiment are crucial. A good problem-solver needs to use any number of techniques and approaches, so you must show flexibility and adaptability. If you come with only one method of working, your methods will look narrow and limited.
- **Consistency**: as well as diversity, you need to show that you can also take an idea and 'run with it'; that you have developed, in some depth, one or more particular projects or themes.
- **Independence**: at degree level, you will need to be able to generate work that is self-directed and independent. Your portfolio, therefore, needs to show that you have developed your own ways of working that haven't been directed solely by your tutors.
- **Critical/contextual studies**: most degree courses have a theoretical element, usually involving written work, so something that shows your ability to write is also important. Interviewers will also need to know that you are interested in the broader context of art and design. You will be asked about practitioners who have influenced or impressed you and exhibitions you've recently visited.

'Finally, it is impossible to quantify the amount and type of work to take to an interview. While you should include a full range of work that isn't over-edited, you should select carefully rather than include absolutely everything you've ever made! Emphasise your most recent work as this is the work that best represents your current concerns. Because it is fresh in your mind, this is also the work you'll be able to talk about with the most enthusiasm.

'The key to your portfolio is its organisation. Have a strong beginning and end, and order your work coherently in projects or subjects, giving most emphasis to recent work. Listen to advice from tutors: they have great expertise in helping students gain university places. For three-dimensional or large-scale work, bring good-quality photographs or slides. Better still, bring originals, but good reproductions will often suffice.'

Sarah Horton, BA (Hons) Course Leader at Norwich University College of Art

'Ideally, we would like to see a portfolio that demonstrates a high level of visual skill, creativity, commitment and self-motivation. We would be looking for evidence of intellectual enquiry and cultural awareness. We would expect you to have completed a Foundation course and the resulting portfolio may include sketchbooks, ideas books, set projects, self-initiated work, finished pieces, work in progress, photographs or three-dimensional work.

'We value a portfolio of work that includes continuity of ideas, and a series of related images that relate to each other in some way. We are interested in your research, thinking and projects that show the development and progression of an idea. We particularly value self-initiated work because it tells us so much about you! Your portfolio should be self-explanatory – it may be viewed initially in your absence. Edit your work and play with the sequencing of images and projects until they unfold in such a way that they tell us who you are and what you think. And, above all, we are looking for potential.'

Debbie Cook, Tutor at the Royal College of Art and International Postgraduate Coordinator at Central Saint Martins

'A portfolio should speak for itself and tell us about your ideas, your passions and your personal approach to working. A commitment to the subject and an engagement with projects should be evident. You need to be self-motivated and have the capacity to work independently and this should be reflected in your portfolio. We are interested in the journey your work takes, your ability to recognise and generate ideas, explore their possibilities and develop them. This process of thinking and working, within a broad cultural context, is crucial. Finally, present your work in a clear and organised way to ensure that it communicates all that you want it to.'

Annette Bellwood, International Academic Coordinator, London College of Communication

WARNING!

On no account even consider 'borrowing' someone else's work for your portfolio. As well as being unethical, you are almost certain to be found out, as the differences in style will be quite obvious to the trained eyes of the interviewers.

Checklist

- Round up your work.
- Check out courses' portfolio specifications.
- Purchase a portfolio.
- Enrol on short courses.
- Review your portfolio.
- Set targets and deadlines.
- Photograph three-dimensional work.
- Label your portfolio.
- Adapt your portfolio to a particular specification.

8 | The interview

This chapter is about how to make the most of your interview. Although the format of the interview will vary from college to college and there are differences between interviewing for a Foundation course and a specialist degree course, the following guidelines will be of help to you. Make sure that you read this chapter in conjunction with Chapter 7.

What is the purpose of the interview?

Interviews are there to help art schools find the most appropriate students and to help students find the most appropriate art schools. Most people who fear interviews do so either because they misunderstand their purpose or because they do not know what to expect and imagine the worst. We worry that we will be asked impossible questions, that the interviewers will not like us or that they will try to catch us out; we worry that we will not be good enough.

Consider this: art schools exist because students want to study art and design. Without the students, there would be no colleges, no lecturers, no admissions tutors and no courses. In other words, where would art schools be without you? You are the single most important element in the educational process and, as such, it is not in any college's interest to make life difficult for you. Yes, interviewers will be trying to find out whether you are suited to the course for which you are applying, and yes, they will be carefully considering both you and your work, and yes, you can expect to be asked some challenging questions – but try to take a positive attitude. Most people are nervous at interview; admissions tutors understand this and will make allowances. They are there to get the best from you.

Also, remember that the interview provides you with an opportunity to assess a prospective college. Hopefully, you will have visited the college before your interview and checked things out, but a second look around will not do you any harm. Since you will probably be studying under some of the people who will be interviewing you, check them out too.

What to expect

The process for interviewing depends on the course and institution you are applying to. In some cases, you may not be interviewed at all; in some, you will deliver your portfolio for consideration prior to being offered an interview; and at others, you leave your portfolio with the admissions tutors on the day of your interview, they initially look at it without you, and then ask you in to discuss it with them – this may be 10 minutes after they take it or sometime later that day.

In many instances, especially at interviews for degree courses, the interview begins with you being asked to present your work briefly to an interviewer or a panel of interviewers who are seeing it for the first time. As you show your work, the conversation will develop into a more formal question-and-answer session. Some institutions, especially those that request the submission of a portfolio online, conduct interviews through an online video call. As interviews vary from college to college, it is best to read the college's literature to try to find out as much as you can about their particular process before attending.

Interviews vary in length from as little as five or 10 minutes to up to 30 or 40 minutes for specialist degree courses. Do not be surprised or worried if the interview feels as if it is very short. Time seems to pass much more rapidly in this kind of situation. Also remember that the interviewers are experts, know what they are looking for, and often, will be able to come to a decision quickly. This is particularly the case for Foundation courses, where admissions tutors will frequently have to see literally hundreds of students in a matter of weeks.

In some cases you will find out if you have been successful on the day, but in most cases you will be notified by letter in due course.

Preparing

It is impossible to know exactly what you will be asked at interview, and in some ways, it is not helpful to be overly prepared since it is much better to allow a discussion to develop naturally, answering the questions that you have been asked rather than insisting that you talk about what you have been reading up on. However, while being over-prepared is one thing, being underprepared is quite another and should be avoided at all costs – it will suggest to the interviewers that you are not really interested in the course. The best way to prepare is to think in general about how you might respond to the specific questions you know that you are likely to be asked. As a guide, consider the following:

- Why have you applied for this particular course?
- Why have you applied to study it here?
- Which artists have influenced you?
- What are you hoping to do in the future?

If you have been conscientious about choosing a course, you will be able to make a positive response to the first two questions. (Make sure that you have read Chapters 2 and 3.) Rereading your notes and personal statement, looking through the course prospectus and talking things through with others will all help. Rather than trying to 'revise' for the answers that you think the interviewers will want, simply remind yourself of what you have done, so that you can respond honestly.

With respect to the question 'Which artists have influenced you?', before going to the interview, look through your work and consider how it relates to that of others. If you have worked on a written project, reread it. Looking through your sketchbooks and scrapbooks can also help, since they are, in part, a record of your creative process. These visual prompts will help to remind you of your influences.

During the period leading up to your interview, make a point of getting out and about. Make sure that you visit some exhibitions. In addition to looking at well-known exhibits in museums, go and see a show of new work. Also, keep up to date by reading the arts pages of national newspapers and periodicals – see the reading list in Chapter 12.

If you are applying for a place on a Foundation course it is likely that your future plans will include taking a degree. You can say this. If you are applying for a place on a specialist degree course, jotting down a few notes to help you think things through may be helpful in preparing for the fourth question, the one about your future plans. Whatever your thoughts might be, do not worry if you cannot come up with a complete answer. That is perfectly normal. It would be a pretty boring world to live in if we all knew exactly what we were going to do in the future! You just need to be able to show the interviewer that you are reflecting on your options and have some possible ideas in mind.

Assuming that you have done your homework and know as much as possible about the course, you will not need to use up valuable time asking questions about course structure or discussing specific issues such as funding. If you are given the chance to ask questions or make comments, it is usually much better to respond to something you have just been discussing with the interviewer than to set your own agenda.

Perhaps the best way to prepare for this is by taking a mock interview, which will give you a feel for how an interview develops. Many schools and colleges offer mock interviews to their own students and, in some cases, to external candidates. If you have the chance to do one, make sure you do not miss out. Mock interviews provide excellent preparation and an excellent way to identify and resolve potential problems.

Discussing your work with art college or university teachers can be a daunting prospect and you will need to practise before your interview. As a general rule of thumb, try to structure any discussion of your work as follows:

1. **Where the idea for the piece came from**: this is an opportunity to talk about artists whose work you like, exhibitions you have visited or previous work that you have produced.
2. **How your ideas were realised in the piece**: you could talk about the composition, the materials and the techniques you used, as well as what the work represents.
3. **Where the work will lead you**: you could talk about what you will work on next, what you might have done differently or how the piece has led you to investigate other artists or techniques.

The interviewer will help you by asking questions and possibly suggesting other areas of research.

Practicalities

As well as thinking about the kind of questions that you might be asked, it is also important to consider a few practicalities. For example, how will you be travelling to the interview? If you are applying to a local art school, you may only have to make a short journey. On the other hand, you may be applying to a course a long way from home, so consider the logistics. In some cases, an overnight stay may be necessary.

Also think about how you intend to transport your work. In many instances you will be able to carry everything in a portfolio. As has been mentioned, most colleges are happy to look at photographs of three-dimensional or larger pieces. However, in some situations (e.g. with pieces under a certain size), it will be necessary to take this work with you. You may need to ask a friend for help or to ask the college for advice. Can you comfortably manage your portfolio or is it too heavy?

Practise your presentation technique. Whether you are an international or home student, your interview may be via an online video call. If your interview is going to be done remotely, make sure you have a good internet connection and that your webcam is of good enough resolution to show your work properly.

The night before

Assuming that you are well organised, there should be nothing left to do except relax and get a good night's sleep, so make sure that you do! Easy to say, difficult to do. We all get nervous before a big day and you might find it difficult to switch off. Don't worry if this happens – it just means that you're normal. Try doing something to take your mind off things, like watching a film, chatting with friends or maybe taking a little gentle exercise, and try not to worry. Be positive. Remember, art schools cannot exist without students!

The interview itself – some tips

- **Make sure you arrive early**: you do not want to be rushing around at the last minute.
- **Dress comfortably**: your interviewers will be far more interested in who you are and what you do than what you wear. If your hair is bright blue and shaved on one side, fine. If it is not, well that's fine too. You will need much more than a good hairstyle to get into art school!
- **Make eye contact**: if you are asked to show your work, don't turn your back on the interviewers; try to position your portfolio between yourself and the people you are speaking to, or, if you are standing side by side, turn towards them from time to time.
- **Be willing to listen as well as talk**: sometimes when we are nervous we talk too much. Try to listen carefully to the questions that you are being asked. You will respond far more intelligently if you understand what has been said. If you do not understand, do not be afraid to ask for further explanation. Sometimes there will be pauses in the conversation. Do not let this unnerve you: the tutors are just concentrating while they look at your work.
- **Understand why you have been asked to attend an interview**: it is because what the university knows about you so far (what you have written in your personal statement, your work that you have submitted in an online application, your academic history or what your teachers have written about you) leads them to believe that you would be a valuable presence at the university or art school, and that you have the potential to become a successful artist, designer or architect. So be confident!
- **Be willing to consider new ideas**: you will be very difficult to teach if you find it hard to keep an open mind. Try not to become defensive if some of your responses to questions are challenged.
- **Try and relax before you walk in**: then, be natural, authentic and believe in yourself.
- **Remember to switch your phone off, or keep it on silent**: you don't want it distracting you or the interviewer.
- **Be yourself**: you do not need to put on an act. Never try to bluff or lie. You will always be found out, so only show your own work and if you do not know something, then say so.
- **Above all, be enthusiastic**: do not be afraid to express your commitment and passion for your subject. You will have worked very hard up to this point. Let your interviewers know that this matters to you. Try not to be cool. Art schools are looking for motivated students.

> **HOPE**
>
> Use the acronym HOPE as a reminder of the personal qualities that you will try to display at interview:
>
> - honesty;
> - open-mindedness;
> - preparedness;
> - enthusiasm.

Meet up with a friend and talk things through; this will help you to put things into perspective. Also, it will greatly help your fellow students if you give them some feedback. They may not have had an interview yet, and your experience will be beneficial. A day or two later, when you have had the chance to reflect a little, make a note of anything that sticks in your mind that might be helpful for the next time.

> 'Before my interview for the Fine Art Photography BA at the Glasgow School of Art, I was thinking about all the different questions they might ask; but when it came to it, it was quite straightforward and they didn't try to catch me out. They asked me to talk about three influences on my work and why the course would suit me, but mostly the interview was about my work. I chose the Glasgow course because the darkroom was very impressive and I could see myself working well there. They asked me about this and the darkroom techniques I was using in my work. I think the interview went well because I could show that I had some intentions going into the course and that I was eager to be proactive.'
>
> Lucy M, BA Fine Art Photography,
Glasgow School of Art

> 'I had one interview for a Foundation course and two for BA Textiles, all of which were successful. The advice I would give you is: be well-prepared, practise interview skills and seek guidance from teachers and tutors. Doing this can significantly improve the chances of success during the portfolio review and interview process. Remember to showcase your passion, creativity and unique artistic perspective.

> 'Building confidence in discussing your work is important and can greatly benefit your interview performance. Ensure that you are familiar with every piece in your portfolio, including the concept, technique and inspiration behind each artwork. Be prepared to discuss why you chose specific pieces, how they showcase your skills and artistic development and what they mean to you personally.

'During interviews, it's not just about the final artwork; interviewers are often interested in understanding your creative process. Be ready to explain the steps you took to create your artwork, from initial ideation to execution. Discuss the materials, techniques and concepts you explored and how they influenced your artistic decisions.

'Be open-minded and receptive to feedback, as it shows your willingness to grow and learn from others. Additionally, reflect on your own artistic journey, acknowledging areas where you want to improve and how the chosen course or future studies can support your growth.

'Practise talking about your artwork in front of different audiences, such as friends, family members or fellow artists. This will help you refine your explanations and become comfortable conveying your artistic vision. Remember to stay authentic, passionate and enthusiastic during your interviews.'

Anna R, Foundation, University of the Arts London

'My preparation for my fashion degree course interview at Bristol UWE included designing a little booklet about the university, to show that I was interested in the university as well as the art campus and course. I knew they would ask me about a designer I liked, so I chose someone not so well known, as I thought everyone else would go mainstream. I made sure that my portfolio included things other than fashion. I was asked why I chose Bristol, and lots of questions about my portfolio such as "Why did you do the stitching like that?". I was very relaxed at the interview because I made a point of being sociable with the other students who were also waiting to be interviewed.

'Even though the degree was a fashion course, I still had to do other things in years 1 and 2, such as textiles. It was only in the third year that I could steer the degree more to my own interests. Preparing my final collection was exhausting and I would fall asleep within seconds of lying down. We were given two hours a week with teachers and pattern cutters but the rest was all down to me. Money was also an issue as we had to buy all of our own materials. The department chose who would show their work, so although the atmosphere was competitive, we still had to cooperate and get on with each other.'

Annabel K, BA Fashion

Admissions tutors' advice for interviews

- *'In interviews, the reviewers are looking for students who demonstrate curiosity about why the world looks like it does.'*
- *'I will expect them to talk about books, journals and shows, and to be able to get under the skin of a subject.'*
- *'Make sure you convince your interviewers that you are passionate about the subject and the particular course you are being interviewed for.'*
- *'When I meet prospective students, I am looking for potential.'*
- *'If you are closed to new ideas, it will be impossible to teach you and your place will be offered to someone else.'*
- *'Interview questions focus on both how and why the work [in the portfolio] was produced and how it might develop.'*
- *'I am not interested in technique – technique can be learned – I am interested in ideas and an open mind.'*
- *'If the student I am interviewing hasn't been to see any exhibitions or shows recently, I tend to doubt their real interest in studying art.'*
- *'Your interviewers are looking for creativity and a willingness to experiment.'*
- *'The internet means that no one, however far from a city, has any excuse not to explore new ideas and get inspiration from practising artists.'*
- *'Be as chatty as you can in your interview. We are looking for good communicators who will share their ideas and not be afraid to discuss their own work.'*
- *'We want to make sure that you are energetic, excited about your future studies and, above all, curious.'*

Checklist

- Visit exhibitions.
- Try to see the work of graduates from the art school, either at degree shows or online.
- Practise talking about your own work.
- Read the arts pages of national newspapers and magazines.
- Review your portfolio.
- Conduct a mock interview.
- Check the interview date, time and location.
- Find out how to get to your interview.

9 | Offers and what to do on results day

You have done all of the hard work – your personal statement, the interview, the examinations – and you are now waiting for your results, the results that will determine whether you have achieved what you need to take your university place. This chapter explains what happens when you get your results, and if you have achieved grades that are either better or worse than expected, what other options are available to you.

When the results are available

- A levels – mid-August;
- IB – early in July;
- Scottish Highers – first week of August.

Ask your school or college for the exact date and time that they will issue you with the results. Whichever of the exam systems you are sitting, you need to act quickly if you:

- have missed the grades or scores that you require to satisfy your firm offer;
- are not holding any offers and wish to apply through UCAS Clearing.

Foundation courses

In most cases, you will receive an unconditional offer. In other words, the college has been convinced by your portfolio and interview, and it wants you. All you have to do then is decide whether you want it! However, please note that in nearly all cases, you will be expected to complete your current programme of study successfully.

If applicants are rejected for Foundation courses, in most cases it's because their portfolios are not strong enough. Under these circumstances, it is often possible to reapply once the portfolio has been strengthened.

Conditional offers

Under some circumstances, you might receive a conditional offer. This normally happens if the college feels that while your work is promising, you are not yet ready to cope with the demands of a Foundation course, or because it requires a particular A level grade or, as an overseas student, you would benefit from help with your language skills or with adapting to UK teaching methods in general. In this situation, you may be asked to attend a summer course. (There is a charge for these courses.)

Accepting an offer

Since there is no centralised system for Foundation course applications (other than local schemes such as that run by the University of the Arts London), it is possible to hold a number of offers simultaneously. In this situation, the best strategy is to keep things simple and not to try to juggle too many balls at one time. When you applied, you had probably already decided which college was your first choice, which was second and so on. If you are lucky enough to get offers from a number of colleges, stick to your original plan and accept the offer from the place where you most want to study. Do not accept offers from everyone just to keep your options open. Talk to your teachers or careers advisers if you are unsure about your best course of action.

What if you are rejected?

If you receive rejections, the first thing to do is to get feedback from the institution. If they reject you it is because they are not completely convinced that studying with them is the best option for you. This may be because they feel that your talents would be better directed towards a different course, discipline or environment. It might be because they think that you are not yet ready (creatively, technically or because of your age) to cope with their course. Once you understand why they are not able to offer you a place, you can focus on alternatives or aim to strengthen the areas that they were concerned about and then reapply. Remember that it is not the 'institution' that is rejecting you, it is someone with a creative or academic background who is looking to allocate the places on the course to the students who, in his or her opinion, would be most suited to that course. If you are rejected and have asked for feedback, then you have a number of options open to you:

- Accept one of the other offers that you may have.
- Make new applications to other art schools.
- Take on board their feedback and reapply once you have addressed their concerns. For example, enrol on some short courses or evening classes, or follow a one-year A level/pre-Foundation course.

Degree courses

You may receive an offer directly from the art school to which you have applied or, if you are applying through UCAS, you will (if all goes to plan) receive offers from more than one college.

What to do if you have no offers: UCAS Extra

If you apply for five courses and either receive no offers or decline all the offers you get, you are eligible for UCAS Extra. Extra operates from the end of February to the beginning of July and allows you to add one additional choice at a time.

To find a course using Extra, use the UCAS search tool and the filter 'Show courses with vacancies'. Next, contact the universities and colleges listed to check if they'll consider you. It's recommended that you call the university to which you want to apply before you add the Extra choice, to check whether there is space on the course and to discuss your suitability. To apply for the new course, you need to add the details to your application.

Your chosen university will consider your application, and, if this is unsuccessful, you can add another Extra choice as long as it's before July. If you have not heard back from the university within 21 days, you can add another Extra choice (again, before July).

Once you have received an offer through Extra, you'll need to either accept or decline it. Ensure that you respond by the date displayed on your homepage, or your offer will be automatically declined.

Don't worry if you don't receive the offer you'd hoped for in UCAS Extra – you can still participate in Clearing.

What to do if things go wrong during the exams

Occasionally, students will underperform in an examination through no fault of their own. This could be through distressing family circumstances (a serious illness to a family member, for example), illness in the run-up to the exam (or during the exam) or unforeseen circumstances such as late arrival to the exam due to problems with public transport. In all cases, you should inform the universities that this has happened to you immediately after the examination. You should, if possible, get your referee to give the details to the universities and provide documentary evidence, such as a letter from your GP.

What to do on results day

You can collect your results from your school or college, or you can arrange to receive them via email or post. It's a good idea to go into school or college to receive them in person, so that you can get support and advice from teachers and careers advisers about your options if you need it.

UCAS receives your exam results directly and will update UCAS Hub with the outcome of your university applications on results day. The system will be busy, so you might need to be patient to find out whether you've been successful.

You'll need to have the following things ready to ensure that you can do everything you might need to on results day:

- UCAS Hub login details;
- UCAS ID number;
- UCAS Clearing number, if you go into Clearing;
- details of your offers;
- the UCAS and Clearing numbers of your chosen universities;
- a working phone and computer, so you can communicate by phone or email.

When you do get your results, one of four things will happen:

1. You receive confirmation of your place from the university you selected as your firm choice and accept it.
2. You have not met the offer from your firm choice, but you will receive confirmation from the university you selected as your insurance choice and accept it.
3. You have met and exceeded the offer made by your firm choice and decide to try to swap courses by going through Clearing (see below).
4. You have not met the requirements of any offers and need to go through Clearing.

If you have achieved the grades that meet the offer made by the university you selected as either your firm choice or insurance choice and are happy with this offer, then congratulations! You do not need to do anything. However, if you want to decline your firm place and make use of UCAS Clearing or have not met any offers and need to use Clearing, then read on.

What to do if you exceeded the grades that you expected

If you have met and exceeded the conditional requirements of your firm choice and it has accepted you – therefore converting the conditional offer into an unconditional one – you could potentially swap your place for one on another course that you prefer by using the 'decline my place' button in the application. The phrase 'met and exceeded' means that if you needed BBB, you would have achieved ABB or better. It doesn't necessarily mean that you just got more UCAS points. For example, if you needed BBB and achieved A*BC, then you would have accumulated more UCAS points with A*BC than you would have if you had only achieved BBB. However, you would have still failed to meet one of your grade requirements. In cases like this, your eligibility will depend on whether your offer was based on UCAS points or grades.

If you decide to pursue a different course, you have to go through UCAS Clearing. Since more than 50,000 students get a course through Clearing, it is highly recommended that you find the course of your preference as soon as possible, as this is a first come, first served system.

Use the Clearing search tool to find all the available courses. Once you have found an alternative course, you will need to phone the university yourself. When you call the university, you will need to give them your UCAS personal ID number and explain straight away that you have exceeded the grades of your offers and are applying through Clearing. Be prepared to answer questions about why you really want to study on that course. If they agree to accept you, and you, in turn, agree to accept them, this will happen during the phone call. Once you receive an offer, you can add it to your application so the college or university can officially accept you. At this stage, your status on UCAS Hub will change. Remember that if you do not find an alternative course that you want, or do not get accepted onto an alternative course, your original firm offer will still stand.

Make sure that you think carefully about the courses and universities if you decide to go through Clearing. Just because a university has higher entry requirements or is considered to be more prestigious, it does not necessarily mean that you will enjoy the course more. Consider carefully why you selected your initial firm choice and check whether your reasons are still valid and you have the same interest and passion to study a new course.

What to do if you have no confirmed offers

If you are not holding any offers, there could be several explanations:

- You may have missed the required grades of both your firm and insurance offers.
- You may have achieved the right grades but not in the right subjects.
- The university or UCAS may not have received your results. The examination boards send the results automatically to UCAS, but if you sat an exam at a different centre, for example, then this may not have happened.
- The examination system that you sat does not automatically send the results to UCAS – for instance, if you sat overseas qualifications.

In the cases of achieving the right grades but not in the right subjects, contact your firm choice university to discuss this with them. Universities may revise their offer and admit you if they still have places, or if you missed the grade by only a few marks, they may ask you to try for a remark. Exam boards change the marks in only a few cases, though, and they can go down or up, so don't place all your hopes on this. If you still do not receive an offer from your firm choice university and have not received an offer from your insurance choice university, then call your insurance choice university. If, by the end of this process, you still have no offers, you will need to enter UCAS Clearing.

UCAS Clearing

Clearing is the name given to the system in which all remaining course vacancies are advertised on the UCAS website and in national newspapers. In Clearing, you contact the universities directly that have publicised course vacancies and give them your grades and UCAS ID number. If you think that you might need to use the Clearing system, it is best to be well-prepared because the vacancies are filled very quickly. Clearing is typically open from July to October.

Alongside their search tool, which includes over 30,000 course options, UCAS also offers Clearing matches, a tool that 'matches' candidates to a list of courses in UCAS Hub. If you find yourself in Clearing, it is advisable to check the 'View matches' button; if you find a course you like, select the 'I'm interested' button. If the university or college still has available places, they will contact you to discuss further and possibly make you an offer.

Advice for Clearing

- Make sure that you have your UCAS ID number and a copy of your UCAS application ready for results day.
- Remain proactive! Use the Clearing matches tool to speed up the process of finding another place.
- You need to have access to a phone that you can use exclusively, as you may need to make a lot of calls over the course of results day.
- You also need to have access to the internet in order to access the directory of courses available through Clearing on the UCAS website. This is particularly useful as the website also has the university contact numbers that you will need to call.
- Think about the option of studying on courses that might not be identical to the one that you originally applied for, but are related.
- Be ready for an impromptu telephone interview. The admissions staff may ask why you want to study on the course, and you will need to have a little bit more tact than just saying 'because I didn't get into the course I really wanted to'. Instead, you could say something like 'Even though I didn't get into my firm or insurance choices, I did apply/intend to apply/visit during the open day/ know that the course has a good student satisfaction rating in the *Guardian* and so on.'

If you decide to retake your A levels

If you have not achieved the grades that you needed for your chosen universities, and you do not want to take the available Clearing places, you could consider retaking one or more A levels. In the days when most examination boards offered January sittings, retaking might have meant studying for one term to boost the grade. The period from January to September could then be used to earn money, gain more work experience or travel the world. But, apart from international A levels, A level exams are now only available in June, and so retaking will involve studying for another year, so you need to be sure that your university aspirations are genuine enough to give you the motivation to add this extra year to your studies. As the A level system is now fully reformed, barring the last Phase Three legacy-subject examinations, you will need to retake the entire two-year qualification again and therefore plan to be able to do this in just a single year – you do not want a repeat of the examination if you are underprepared.

Speak to your teachers about the implications of retaking your exams. Some independent sixth form colleges provide specialist advice and teaching for students. Interviews to discuss this are free and carry no obligation to enrol on a course, so it is worth taking the time to talk to their staff before you embark on A level retakes. Many further education colleges also offer retake courses, and some schools will allow students to return to resit subjects, either as external examination candidates or by repeating a year.

If you decide to reapply

Universities are usually happy to consider students who are reapplying, either because they did not get the required grades first time around, or because they did not receive any offers of places. It is worth contacting the university to check whether this is the case. Some will have policies on grade requirements for retake candidates, while others might ask for evidence of any extenuating circumstances that may have affected the previous application.

> **TIP!**
>
> If there were extenuating circumstances that affected your application, include a brief mention of this in the personal statement ('I was disappointed not to have achieved the required grades, because my studies were affected by illness, but this has made me even more determined to become an engineer') but leave the details to the referee.
>
> If you are retaking, you can use the extra term or extra year to add weight to your application, for example, by gaining more work experience, taking up a new subject, enrolling in evening classes that are relevant to your application and furthering your reading.

10 | Fees and funding

If you are planning on studying at a college or university, you need to think about what it will cost you to do so. For some further education courses, UK students who are below an age threshold will not have to pay tuition fees, but in almost all circumstances, you will need to pay for higher education and postgraduate courses.

UK (home) students

Foundation courses

Foundation courses are classed as further education courses, rather than higher education. For this reason, student loans are not available. However, students from the UK who are under 19 years old on 31 August in the year that the course starts are eligible for free tuition. Students who do not come into this category may have to pay tuition fees, which are likely to be about £5,260–£7,400 per year depending on where you study.

Degree and HND courses

As the government of each of the UK home nations sets the fees that universities can charge, the tuition fee that you will have to pay for undergraduate courses will depend on where you live and where you intend to study. In England, only universities with a Teaching Excellence Framework (TEF) award and an access and participation plan (APP) from the Office for Students (OfS) are permitted to charge the maximum tuition fee. However, the TEF's impact on tuition fees is specific to England: it does not affect fee caps in Scotland, Wales or Northern Ireland.

In the autumn of 2025, the UK government announced that, from 2026/27, university tuition fees in England are set to increase every year in line with inflation. The tuition fee cap for Welsh students is also set to rise for the 2026/27 academic year, with future increases to be confirmed at a later date. At the time of writing, Scotland and Northern Ireland are yet to confirm any changes to tuition fees in 2026 and beyond.

There are a number of variations between the systems in England, Scotland, Wales and Northern Ireland, which can result in significant differences between the fees that are ultimately paid by students. For reference, this is the current situation regarding tuition fees:

10| Fees and Funding

- Students from England will be required to pay maximum fees of £9,790 for 2026/27, rising to £10,050 for 2027/28.
- Students from Wales will be required to pay maximum fees of £9,790 for 2026/27, with increases in subsequent academic years yet to be confirmed.
- Students from Scotland who study at Scottish universities are not required to pay tuition fees. However, Scottish students who choose to study in other UK nations are required to pay the tuition fees set by that country.
- Students living in Northern Ireland paid up to £4,855 to study in Northern Ireland in 2025/26. Northern Irish students who choose to study in other UK nations are required to pay the tuition fees set by that country.

EU students

EU students are charged the same fees as charged to non-EU international students, which are significantly higher than those charged to UK students and are determined by each university. Some students from the EU may be eligible for some support in terms of student loans from the UK government, but this is dependent on a number of factors, so it is best to check personal eligibility. Students from the Republic of Ireland are exempt from paying higher fees and are eligible for home fee status.

Living expenses

Your living expenses include the cost of your accommodation, food, clothes, travel and equipment, leisure and social activities – plus possible extras like field trips and study visits.

Check university and college websites for information about possible living costs. Some offer more detailed advice than others and give breakdowns under various headings such as accommodation, food and daily travel. Others go even further and give typical weekly, monthly or annual spends.

If you're living away from home, accommodation will make up the largest proportion of your living costs. There is likely to be a range of accommodation options – from a standard room in university halls through to privately rented accommodation – with a range of price points. You'll probably be surprised when you do some research to find that the cheapest and most expensive towns are not as you might have expected; the cost of accommodation often depends on how much of it is available in a particular area.

When choosing accommodation, it is essential to consider its location and factor in the cost of travel to your university or college. It is also important to find out what's included in the accommodation costs (such as utilities, personal property insurance and Wi-Fi) and whether it is possible to pay for accommodation during term time only.

Funding your studies

How do you fund your time in higher education? Don't ignore this question and leave it until the last minute! You will need to think carefully about how to budget for several years' costs – and you need to know what help you might get from:

- the government;
- your family or partner;
- paid part-time work;
- other sources, such as bursaries and scholarships.

This chapter gives a brief overview of a complicated funding situation, which can vary according to where you come from and where you plan to study. For more details about the different types of funding available and how to apply for them, check your regional student finance website:

- www.gov.uk/contact-student-finance-england
- www.saas.gov.uk
- www.studentfinanceni.co.uk
- www.studentfinancewales.co.uk

Tuition fee loans

For UK students, tuition fees can be covered by taking out a tuition fee loan, which will be paid directly to your university or college at the start of each year of your course. You are effectively given a loan by the government that you repay through your income tax after you finish your course but only once your earnings reach a certain threshold. For 2026/27, these income thresholds stand at:

- £25,000 per year for students from England (Plan 5);
- £29,385 a year for students from Wales (Plan 2);
- £33,795 for students from Scotland (who go to university outside of Scotland) (Plan 4);
- £26,900 for students from Northern Ireland (Plan 1).

(All figures apply to students starting their course after 1 August 2023.)

You only start repayments once you are earning over this threshold. In addition, any outstanding balance on your loan will be cancelled after a certain period of time if you have not already cleared it in full. The length of time depends on the rules at the time you took out the loan. For students in England who started their studies in September 2023, the repayment period was extended to 40 years (from 30 years), so it is recommended that students in other regions keep a close eye on any developments with respect to the length of the loan repayment period. At the time of writing, the loan repayment term is 30 years for students from Wales and Scotland, and 25 years for students from Northern Ireland.

Loan repayments are set at 9% of anything you earn over the annual income threshold.

The interest rate charged on student loans depends on what repayment plan you are on, but for students in England on Plan 5 it is currently 3.2%.

Maintenance loans

In addition to a tuition fee loan, all students can apply for a maintenance or living cost loan, which is repayable in the same way. All students are entitled to a maintenance loan; however, the amount you can borrow will be dependent on your household income – in other words, it is means-tested. 'Household income' refers to your family's gross annual income (their income before tax). With the exception of loans available to Scottish students, the amount you can claim also varies depending on your living situation, with the maximum loan being available to students living away from home in London.

Each regional student finance website includes a finance calculator tool that will give an estimate of the finance you would be eligible for based on your family income and other factors, and it is well worth looking at this before planning your budget.

The UK government has announced that, from the 2026/27 academic year, maintenance loans for students from England will increase in line with inflation. Maintenance loans for Welsh students are also increasing; however, details of any additional support for students from Scotland and Northern Ireland for the 2026/27 academic year are yet to be confirmed. For reference, a summary of the current maintenance support arrangements is given below.

England (2026/27)
The maximum annual maintenance loan in England:

- £9,118 for those living in the family home;
- £10,830 for those living away from home (£14,135 in London).

Wales (2026/27)
In Wales, students can get a combination of a maintenance grant, which they do not have to pay back, and a maintenance loan. Although the grants are means-tested, most students should get a grant of at least £1,020.

The maximum amounts for maintenance loans and grants in Wales:

- £10,685 for those living in the family home;
- £12,590 for those living away from home (£15,720 in London).

Scotland (2025/26)

In Scotland, students can get a mix of maintenance loans and non-repayable bursaries (grants) to cover living expenses. These are as follows (all figures per year):

- household income up to £20,999: £2,000 bursary and £7,000 loan;
- household income £21,000–£23,999: £1,125 bursary and £7,000 loan;
- household income £24,000–£33,999: £500 bursary and £7,000 loan;
- household income £34,000 and above: no bursary and £6,000 loan.

Unlike the rest of the UK, household income for Scottish students is measured on the income bands listed above rather than exact household income.

In addition, a Special Support Loan of £2,400 is also available to all full-time students. Unlike the maintenance loan and bursary, this is not means-tested, but it is repayable.

Northern Ireland (2025/26)

The maximum annual maintenance loan in Northern Ireland:

- £6,300 for those living in the family home;
- £8,132 for those living away from home (£11,391 in London).

In addition, you may be eligible for a non-repayable maintenance grant if your household income is below £41,065. This is paid alongside any maintenance loan you qualify for and is up to £3,475.

Postgraduate courses

There are Postgraduate Master's Loans available to home students, Irish students and EU students who have been granted settled status. Eligibility criteria and the amounts awarded differ across the regions of the UK, so it is important to check with the student loans organisations of your chosen region to see if you are eligible and how much you might be granted. For example, in England you may be awarded a maximum of £12,858, which is to contribute to tuition fees and living costs. In Wales, the maximum amount is £19,225 and in Northern Ireland, the maximum amount awarded is £6,500 (all figures are for the 2025/26 academic year). These loans are repayable after the end of your course, alongside any student loans for undergraduate study.

The Master of Architecture (MArch) is treated differently from most other postgraduate courses. If you are studying a full-time MArch that is eligible for undergraduate student finance (as many Part 2 architecture courses are), you should apply for undergraduate funding. You can only use the Postgraduate Master's Loan for a MArch if the course is part-time or it is not eligible for undergraduate funding.

Postgraduate students are often self-funded or may be assisted by scholarships from universities or from other organisations. Contacting the institution to which you are applying is a good way to begin exploring your options. See Appendix 1 for telephone numbers, emails and web addresses.

The Turing Scheme

Following the UK's withdrawal from the European Union, the Erasmus+ scheme has been replaced by the Turing Scheme.

UK educational institutions are able to apply to the Turing Scheme for funding, which they then use to offer educational and training opportunities around the world to students (participating students don't have to be UK nationals). It's worth researching whether an institution you are interested in offers this possibility and what kinds of projects it engages with.

Other sources of funding

Commercial organisations, charitable trusts, educational institutions and government agencies all offer sponsorship, special grants, access funds and scholarships. If you are facing financial difficulties, a good place to start looking for information is the college to which you are applying. For example, Edinburgh College of Art offers the Andrew Grant Postgraduate Scholarships (worth £13,000) to those studying on postgraduate courses. There are a number of similar sources of support available at institutions throughout the UK. You should look at the funding sections on the institutions' websites for further information. Remember that these scholarships vary in size and availability from year to year, so you should check the websites regularly for updates.

The Arts and Humanities Research Council (AHRC) also offers some funding for art and design students. Contact details can be found in Chapter 12 of this book.

For architecture students, RIBA offers a number of awards and scholarships to students in Part 1 or Part 2 studies (see Chapter 4) and to graduates who are gaining more practical experience. The RIBA Hardship Funds are awarded to students who might not otherwise be able to study architecture or to continue their studies. RIBA also administers postgraduate scholarships, travel scholarships and research scholarships. Details can be found on the RIBA website.

11 | Postgraduate courses

Having completed your degree, you can continue your studies, choosing from the wide variety of postgraduate courses that are available. Postgraduate courses allow you either to specialise in a particular field that interests you or to reach a higher academic level to widen your job opportunities. Applications can be made either in the final year of your degree or after you have graduated and completed a period of professional practice.

Types of course

When considering whether or not to apply for postgraduate study, your first choices will be between a higher degree, diploma and certificate and between a taught and a research programme. Courses, which vary in structure, include one-, two- and three-year postgraduate degrees, leading, for example, to the award of a Master of Arts (MA), and postgraduate certificates and diplomas that prepare students for specific professions, such as a Postgraduate Certificate in Animation, a Postgraduate Diploma in Museum Studies or a PGCE, the teaching qualification. You will also be able to develop a career in research, with a PhD or MPhil (see below for details) being the starting point.

Postgraduate courses are available at many colleges, art schools and universities. Many institutions offer courses at both undergraduate and postgraduate levels, making it possible to remain within the same institution for all your studies. There are also specialist schools of art such as the Royal College of Art and the Royal Academy Schools of Art which offer only postgraduate courses.

Master's degrees

Master's courses used to last for one year and the majority were organised as taught programmes. However, there are now numerous two-year courses. It is now also possible to do a master's degree by research – usually leading to a Master of Philosophy (or MPhil). This is a higher-level qualification than an MA but below a doctorate.

Taught master's degrees usually take from nine to 12 months (or two years if you are a part-time student). The first six to nine months are usually studio and classroom based, and are followed by time spent on a research project.

Doctorates

A Doctor of Philosophy (PhD) is always achieved by research under the guidance of a supervisor – a member of academic staff who shares your interest and is an expert in that particular area. Your area of study will be highly specialised, and you will have to submit a thesis – of up to 100,000 words – based on original research. A PhD typically takes four years (but can take longer).

Courses cover the full range of art and design disciplines and, while it is usual to continue working within the same area of study that you have followed at undergraduate level, it is also possible to cross over into other areas.

Applying for a postgraduate course

There is no centralised system like UCAS for postgraduate courses, nor is there a set closing date. UCAS does have a postgraduate application system, but not all universities are represented. Details can be found on the UCAS website, www.ucas.com/postgraduate/choosing-postgraduate-course. Some taught programmes have deadlines, but it is often possible to begin a research programme at different points during the academic year. There may, in fact, be different starting dates throughout the year for all types of courses – but the autumn term is still the most popular. There is no limit to the number of applications that you may make, but most students make a maximum of six applications and on average around two to three.

Application procedures vary, but in the first instance, you should refer to the college at which you intend to study. You will be required to submit a portfolio, attend an interview and, in some cases, present a formal proposal of an intended programme of study. Take a look at the comments below from Andrew Watson to get an idea of how one college approaches the admissions process.

> 'Postgraduate courses have well-defined portfolio requirements. These will vary in relation to the level of postgraduate study (Postgraduate Certificate, Postgraduate Diploma and MA) and in relation to the subject area (design, art, media). Start by checking the published portfolio requirements for the course you are applying to. The portfolio is used as a means of assessing an applicant's suitability for the level of study and their motivation and potential to achieve the course aims and learning outcomes. At postgraduate level, you should be able to demonstrate intelligence and maturity

of approach to a personal area of interest as well as confidence in the abilities that you will require to explore a range of technical and formal problems. You should also emphasise your ability to undertake independent research. For design-based studies, it is important to show that you can produce, communicate and evaluate a range of ideas and design responses to a particular problem. MA applicants should be able to show critical and analytical abilities and evidence of original thinking. Fine art and media courses would expect the applicant to be able to show, either at interview or in an accompanying statement, an awareness of the cultural and social context of the work submitted in the portfolio.

'Many courses now limit the quantity and form of the work submitted at application and ask for additional examples to be shown at interview. Again, it is very important to check specific published course requirements on this.'

Andrew Watson, Course Director for the
Postgraduate Certificate in Professional Studies in
Art and Design, Central Saint Martins

'My MA in Textiles Mixed Media Design at the Royal College of Art (RCA) allowed me to gain a greater understanding of myself as a creative practitioner. It introduced me to many people from all walks of life who have interests like mine, and these connections have been invaluable.

'I was able to find myself as a practitioner in a highly professional and creative environment, and the college introduced us to well-regarded people from the design industries to help better our work and our understanding of design.

'I took part in a series of competitions while studying at the RCA, and we were offered incredible opportunities to present our work to the public as well as artists, which created a fabtastic platform for from which we could launch our careers.'

Jess Z, MA Textiles Mixed Media Design,
Royal College of Art

Advice on choosing and applying for postgraduate courses

- Have a clear idea of what you want to achieve by enrolling on a postgraduate course: are you aiming to develop your practice in a more general way, or are you looking to specialise in a particular area within your chosen field? You will need to decide what you want the outcome to be before choosing which courses to apply for.
- If you are thinking about postgraduate courses because you want to teach within a college or university environment, talk to teachers or lecturers about which courses are most appropriate.

11| Postgraduate Courses

- Many postgraduate students choose their courses because they want to work within a specialised field. For example, by specialising in documentary photography having completed a BA in Photography. Try to find out where graduates from your chosen course end up working, and make sure that your own career plans can be realised by taking the course.
- Talk to the course director before making a final decision to find out what type of students follow the course. Are they recent graduates, or industry professionals looking to extend their skills? Will there be other students with the same experience, qualifications or goals as you?
- Do as much research as you can on who will be teaching you and who will be interviewing you, so that you can tailor your portfolio appropriately.

12 | Further information

Applications

Degree courses

UCAS
Rosehill
New Barn Lane
Cheltenham
GL52 3LZ
Tel: 0371 468 0468
www.ucas.com

University of Cambridge
Admissions Office
University of Cambridge
Student Services Centre
New Museums Site
Cambridge
CB2 3PT
Tel: 01223 333308
www.cao.cam.ac.uk

University of Oxford
Undergraduate Admissions Office
University Offices
Wellington Square
Oxford
OX1 2JD
Tel: 01865 270000
www.ox.ac.uk

Books

HEAP 2027: University Degree Course Offers: The Essential Guide to Winning Your Place at University, Brian Heap (Trotman)
How to Complete Your UCAS Application: 2027 Entry, Ryan Moran & UCAS (Trotman)

Funding

UCAS student finance information
www.ucas.com/ucas/undergraduate/finance-and-support

Student Loans Company (SLC)
Tel: 0300 100 0607
www.slc.co.uk

Arts and Humanities Research Council (AHRC)
www.ahrc.ac.uk/funding/opportunities/current

International students

British Council
www.britishcouncil.org

English UK
www.englishuk.com

UK Council for International Student Affairs (UKCISA)
www.ukcisa.org.uk

International English Language Testing System (IELTS)
www.ielts.org

Test of English as a Foreign Language (TOEFL)
www.ets.org/toefl

Art and design bodies

Arts councils

Arts Council England
Brooklands
24 Brooklands Avenue
Cambridge
CB2 8BU
www.artscouncil.org.uk

Arts Council of Wales
Bute Place
Cardiff
CF10 5AL
https://arts.wales

Arts Council of Northern Ireland
Linden Hill House
23 Lindenhall Street
Lisburn
BT28 1FJ
www.artscouncil-ni.org

Creative Scotland
Waverley Gate
2 – 4 Waterloo Place
Edinburgh
EH1 3EG
www.creativescotland.com

Professional bodies

The Association of Photographers
Click Studios
Heritage Court
Cherryduck Studios
8 – 10 Sampson St
London
E1W 1NA
www.the-aop.org

British Film Institute
Belvedere Road
Lambeth
London
SE1 8XT
www.bfi.org.uk

Crafts Council
44a Pentonville Road
London
N1 9BY
www.craftscouncil.org.uk

Design Council
Eagle House
167 City Road
London
EC1V 1AW
www.designcouncil.org.uk

12| Further Information

Printmakers Council
Ground Floor
Unit 23
Blue Anchor Lane
London
SE16 3UL
www.printmakerscouncil.com

Architecture

Architects Registration Board
8 Weymouth Street
London
W1W 5BU
www.arb.org.uk

Royal Institute of British Architects (RIBA)
66 Portland Place
London
W1B 1AD
www.riba.org/

The RIBA President's Medals Student Awards
www.presidentsmedals.com

Reading list

The art schools' and universities' websites and brochures often highlight books that they recommend for students. As you will see if you go to online booksellers or visit good bookshops, there are many thousands of books about art, architecture or design. So, where do you start? The following titles are our personal favourites:

What Are You Looking At?: 150 Years of Modern Art in the Blink of an Eye, Will Gompertz (Viking)

Seven Days in the Art World, Sarah Thornton (Granta Books)

How to Read Paintings, Liz Rideal (Bloomsbury Visual Arts)

The Story of Architecture, Jonathan Glancey (Dorling Kindersley)

Modernism, Richard Weston (Phaidon Press)

A Cultural History of Fashion in the 20th and 21st Centuries, Bonnie English (Bloomsbury Academic)

Photography: A Concise History, Ian Jeffrey (Thames & Hudson)

Art Photography Now, Susan Bright (Thames & Hudson)

The Pot Book, Edmund de Waal and Claudia Clare (Phaidon Press)

The Craftsman, Richard Sennett (Penguin)
Graphic Design Visionaries, Caroline Roberts (Laurence King)
Ways of Seeing, John Berger (Penguin)
The Story of Art, E H Gombrich (Phaidon Press)
The Shock of The New, Robert Hughes (Thames & Hudson)
Drawing on Right Side of the Brain, Betty Edwards (Souvenir Press)
Art on My Mind: Visual Politics, bell hooks (Penguin)

Magazines

This list only scrapes the surface of the publications available. The best places to look for art and design magazines are museum and gallery bookshops, which carry wide selections.

Architects' Journal;
Architectural Review;
Art Monthly;
Artist Portfolio Magazine;
ArtReview;
B&W (photography);
Blueprint (design);
British Journal of Photography;
Ceramic Review;
Ceramics Monthly;
Computer Arts Magazine;
Creative Review;
Frieze;
IMA Magazine (Photography);
Modern Painters;
Next Level;
Photography Monthly;
TATE ETC.

Websites

The internet's shifting landscape means that new sites devoted to art and design appear on a daily basis. We have listed some interesting sites below, but you should also do your own searching when you have free time. Searching for 'art magazine online', for example, will give you over a million starting points.

Aesthetica art magazine: www.aestheticamagazine.com
A List Apart (web design): www.alistapart.com
Art UK:www.artuk.org
Artnet: www.artnet.com
Frieze: www.frieze.com
Google Arts and Culture: https://artsandculture.google.com/
Hyperallergic: www.hyperallergic.com
It's Nice That: www.itsnicethat.com
Juxtapoz Art & Culture Magazine: www.juxtapoz.com
The Museum of Modern Art: www.moma.org
This is Colossal: www.thisiscolossal.com
NY Arts: www.nyartsmagazine.net

12| Further Information

Printmakers' resources and links: www.printmaker.com/links.html
Tate Collection: www.tate.org.uk/art
Whitehot: www.whitehotmagazine.com

Artists' websites

Geraint Evans: www.geraintevans.net
Fergus Hare: www.fergushare.net
Greg Ioannou: www.gregoristomazou.com; @ioannougreg
Anna Lytridou: www.annalytridou.com
Michael Milloy: @michael.milloy
Lucy Mullican: www.lucymullican.com
Johanna Parv: www.johannaparv.com

Appendix 1: Institution contact details

Aberystwyth University
Tel: 01970 622021
Email: ug-admissions@aber.ac.uk
www.aber.ac.uk

Accrington & Rossendale College
Tel: 01254 389933
Email: admissions@nelsongroup.ac.uk
www.accross.ac.uk

Activate Learning (Oxford, Reading, Banbury & Bicester)
Tel: 0800 612 6008
Email: HE@activatelearning.ac.uk
www.activatelearning.ac.uk

Anglia Ruskin University
Tel: 01245 686868
Email: answers@aru.ac.uk
www.aru.ac.uk

University of the Arts London
Email: admissions@arts.ac.uk
www.arts.ac.uk

Arts University Bournemouth
Tel: 01202 363228
Email: admissions@aub.ac.uk
www.aub.ac.uk

Bangor University
Tel: 01248 383717
Email: admissions@bangor.ac.uk
www.bangor.ac.uk

Barking and Dagenham College
Tel: 020 3667 0265
Email: admissions@bdc.ac.uk
www.barkingdagenhamcollege.ac.uk

Barnet and Southgate College
Tel: 020 8266 4000
Email: info@barnetsouthgate.ac.uk
www.barnetsouthgate.ac.uk

Barnfield College, Luton
Tel: 01582 569555
Email: admissions@barnfield.ac.uk
www.barnfield.ac.uk

Barnsley College
Tel: 01226 216216
Email: omlreception@barnsley.ac.uk
www.barnsley.ac.uk

Basingstoke College of Technology
Tel: 01256 306679
Email: nextyear@bcot.ac.uk
www.bcot.ac.uk

University of Bath
Tel: 01225 383019
Email: admissions@bath.ac.uk
www.bath.ac.uk/admissions

Appendix 1: Institution Contact Details

Bath College
Tel: 01225 312191
Email: info@bathcollege.ac.uk
www.bathcollege.ac.uk

Bath Spa University
Tel: 01225 876180
Email: admissions@bathspa.ac.uk
www.bathspa.ac.uk

Bedford College
Tel: 0345 658 8990
www.bedfordcollegegroup.ac.uk

University of Bedfordshire
Tel: 01582 743500
Email: admission@beds.ac.uk
www.beds.ac.uk

Bexley College
Tel: 020 5954 4000
Email: studenthub@lsec.ac.uk
www.lsec.ac.uk

Birmingham City University
Tel: 0121 331 6295
www.bcu.ac.uk

Birmingham Metropolitan College
Tel: 0121 446 4545
Email: he@bmetc.ac.uk
www.bmetc.ac.uk

Bishop Burton College
Tel: 01964 553000
Email: enquiries@bishopburton.ac.uk
www.bishopburton.ac.uk

Blackburn College
Tel: 01254 292929
Email: admissions@blackburn.ac.uk
www.blackburn.ac.uk

Blackpool and The Fylde College
Tel: 01253 504322
Email: admissions@blackpool.ac.uk
www.blackpool.ac.uk

Bournemouth and Poole College
Tel: 01202 205205
Email: enquiries@thecollege.co.uk
www.thecollege.co.uk

Bournemouth University
Tel: 01202 961916
Email: askbu@bournemouth.ac.uk
www.bournemouth.ac.uk

Bradford College
Tel: 01274 088088
Email: admissions@bradfordcollege.ac.uk
www.bradfordcollege.ac.uk

Bridgend College
Tel: 01656 302251
Email: hello@bridgend.ac.uk
www.bridgend.ac.uk

University of Brighton
Tel: 01273 644644
Email: admissions@brighton.ac.uk
www.brighton.ac.uk

Bridgwater and Taunton College
Tel: 01278 455464
Email: info@somerset.ac.uk
www.somerset.ac.uk

City of Bristol College
Tel: 0117 3125000
Email: enquiries@cityofbristol.ac.uk
www.cityofbristol.ac.uk

Brunel University London
Tel: 01895 274000
www.brunel.ac.uk

The University of Buckingham
Tel: 01280 820227
Email: admissions@buckingham.ac.uk
www.buckingham.ac.uk

Buckinghamshire College Group
Tel: 01296 588599
Email: admissions@buckscollegegroup.ac.uk
www.buckscollegegroup.ac.uk

Buckinghamshire New University
Tel: 01494 605060
Email: admissions@bucks.ac.uk
www.bucks.ac.uk

Bury College
Tel: 0161 280 8200
Email: admissions@burycollege.ac.uk
www.burycollege.ac.uk

Calderdale College
Tel: 01422 399316
Email: admissions@calderdale.ac.uk
www.calderdale.ac.uk

University of Cambridge
Email: admissions@cam.ac.uk
www.study.cam.ac.uk

Cambridge School of Visual & Performing Arts
Tel: 01223 341300
Email: admissions@csvpa.com
www.csvpa.com

Capital City College
Tel: 0207 8325000
Email: admissions@capitalccg.ac.uk
www.capitalccg.ac.uk

Canterbury Christ Church University
Tel: 01227 926000
Email: courses@canterbury.ac.uk
www.canterbury.ac.uk

Canterbury College
Tel: 01227 811111
Email: iag@eastkent.ac.uk
www.ekcgroup.ac.uk/colleges/canterbury-college

Cardiff University
Tel: 029 2087 9999
www.cardiff.ac.uk

Cardiff Metropolitan University
Tel: 029 2041 6070
Email: askadmissions@cardiffmet.ac.uk
www.cardiffmet.ac.uk

Carshalton College
Tel: 020 8544 4444
Email: admissions.carshalton@stcg.ac.uk
www.carshalton.ac.uk

Cheshire College South & West
Tel: 01270 654654
Email: info@ccsw.ac.uk
www.ccsw.ac.uk

University of Chester
Tel: 01244 511000
Email: admissions@chester.ac.uk
www.chester.ac.uk

Appendix 1: Institution Contact Details

Chesterfield College
Tel: 01246 500500
Email: admissions@chesterfield.ac.uk
www.chesterfield.ac.uk

University of Chichester
Tel: 01243 816002
Email: admissions@chi.ac.uk
www.chi.ac.uk

Chichester College
Tel: 01243 786321
Email: info@chichester.ac.uk
www.chichester.ac.uk

City College Plymouth
Tel: 01752 305300
Email: info@cityplym.ac.uk
www.cityplym.ac.uk

City of Glasgow College
Tel: 0141 375 5555
Email: enquiries@cityofglasgow.ac.uk
www.cityofglasgowcollege.ac.uk

The City of Liverpool College
Tel: 0151 252 3000
Email: enquiry@liv-coll.ac.uk
www.liv-coll.ac.uk

City of Westminster College
Tel: 020 7723 8826
Email: customer.services@cwc.ac.uk
www.cwc.ac.uk

City of Wolverhampton College
Tel: 01902 836000
www.wolvcoll.ac.uk

Colchester Institute
Tel: 01206 712777
www.colchester.ac.uk

Cornwall College
Tel: 01209 617698
www.cornwall.ac.uk

Coventry University
Tel: 024 7765 2222
Email: ukadmissions@coventry.ac.uk
www.coventry.ac.uk

Craven College
Tel: 01756 791411
Email: customerservices@craven-college.ac.uk
www.craven-college.ac.uk

University for the Creative Arts (UCA)
Tel: 01252 918291
Email: enquiries@uca.ac.uk
www.uca.ac.uk

Croydon College
Tel: 020 8686 5700
Email: admissions@croydon.ac.uk
www.croydon.ac.uk

University of Cumbria
Tel: 01228 588 588
Email: enquirycentre@cumbria.ac.uk
www.cumbria.ac.uk

De Montfort University (Leicester)
Tel: 0116 250 6070
Email: enquiry@dmu.ac.uk
www.dmu.ac.uk

University of Derby
Tel: 01332 591167
Email: askadmissions@derby.ac.uk
www.derby.ac.uk

Doncaster College
Tel: 0800 358 7575
Email: dcinfocentre@don.ac.uk
www.don.ac.uk

Dudley College of Technology
Tel: 01384 363333
Email: admissions@dudleycol.ac.uk
www.dudleycol.ac.uk

University of Dundee
Tel: 01382 383838
www.dundee.ac.uk/study/ug

University of East Anglia (UEA)
Tel: 01603 591515
Email: admissions@uea.ac.uk
www.uea.ac.uk

University of East London (UEL)
Tel: 020 8223 3333
Email: study@uel.ac.uk
www.uel.ac.uk

East Riding College
Tel: 0345 120 0044
Email: admissions@eastridingcollege.ac.uk
www.eastridingcollege.ac.uk

East Surrey College
Tel: 01737 772611
Email: clientservices@esc.ac.uk
www.esc.ac.uk

East Sussex College
Tel: 030 3003 9699
www.escg.ac.uk

The University of Edinburgh
Tel: 0131 650 1000
Email: sra.enquiries@ed.ac.uk
www.ed.ac.uk

Edinburgh Napier University
Tel: 0333 900 6040
Email: studentrecruitment@napier.ac.uk
www.napier.ac.uk

Exeter College
Tel: 01392 400500
Email: info@exe-coll.ac.uk
www.exe-coll.ac.uk/he

Falmouth University
Tel: 01326 213730
Email: applicantservices@falmouth.ac.uk
www.falmouth.ac.uk/admissions

University Centre Farnborough
Tel: 01252 407028
Email: admissions@farn-ct.ac.uk
www.farn-ct.ac.uk

Furness College
Tel: 01229 8250117
Email: info@furness.ac.uk
www.furness.ac.uk

Gateshead College
Tel: 0191 490 2246
Email: start@gateshead.ac.uk
www.gateshead.ac.uk

Glasgow Caledonian University
Tel: 0141 331 8630
Email: studentenquiries@gcu.ac.uk
www.gcu.ac.uk

The Glasgow School of Art
Tel: 0141 353 4500
Email: admissions@gsa.ac.uk
www.gsa.ac.uk

The University of Gloucestershire
Tel: 03330 141414
Email: admissions@glos.ac.uk
www.glos.ac.uk

Appendix 1: Institution Contact Details

Gloucestershire College
Tel: 0345 155 2020
Email: info@gloscol.ac.uk
www.gloscol.ac.uk

Goldsmiths, University of London
Tel: 020 7919 7171
Email: admissions@gold.ac.uk
www.gold.ac.uk

Gower College Swansea
Tel: 01792 284000
Email: enquiries@gcs.ac.uk
www.gowercollegeswansea.ac.uk

Greater Brighton Metropolitan College
Tel: 01273 667704
Email: admissions@gbmc.ac.uk
www.gbmc.ac.uk

University of Greater Manchester
Tel: 01204 900600
Email: enquiries@bolton.ac.uk
www.greatermanchester.ac.uk

University of Greenwich
Tel: 020 8331 9000
Email: courseinfo@gre.ac.uk
www.gre.ac.uk

University Centre Grimsby
Tel: 01472 311222
Email: infocent@grimsby.ac.uk
www.grimsby.ac.uk

Guildford College
Tel: 0800 612 6008
Email: admission@guilford.edu
www.guildford.activelearning.ac.uk

Harrogate College
Tel: 01423 879400
Email: contact@harrogate-college.ac.uk
www.harrogate.ac.uk

Heart of Worcestershire College
Tel: 01905 743456
Email: admissions-worcester@howcollege.ac.uk
www.howcollege.ac.uk

Hereford College of Arts
Tel: 01432 273359
Email: enquiries@hca.ac.uk
www.hca.ac.uk

Heriot-Watt University, Edinburgh
Tel: 0131 4495111
Email: student-services-UK@hw.ac.uk
www.hw.ac.uk

University of Hertfordshire
Tel: 01707 284800
Email: ask@herts.ac.uk
www.herts.ac.uk

University of the Highlands and Islands
Tel: 01463 279190
Email: info@uhi.ac.uk
www.uhi.ac.uk

The University of Huddersfield
Tel: 01484 422288
Email: study@hud.ac.uk
www.hud.ac.uk

Hugh Baird College
Tel: 0151 353 4444
Email: enquiries@hughbaird.ac.uk
www.hughbaird.ac.uk/index.php/university-centre

The University of Hull
Tel: 01482 466100
Email: admissions@hull.ac.uk
www.hull.ac.uk

Hull College
Tel: 01482 329943
Email: info@hull-college.ac.uk
www.hull-college.ac.uk/HE

The University of Kent
Tel: 01227 764000
www.kent.ac.uk

Kingston College
Tel: 020 8546 2151
Email: info.kingston@stcg.ac.uk.
www.stcg.ac.uk

Kingston University
Tel: 020 3308 9932
Email: admissionssops@kingston.ac.uk
www.kingston.ac.uk

Kirklees College
Tel: 01484 437000
Email: info@kirkleescollege.ac.uk
www.kirkleescollege.ac.uk

KLC School of Design (London)
Tel: 020 7376 3377
Email: info@klc.co.uk
www.klc.co.uk

Lakes College – West Cumbria
Tel: 01946 839300
Email: info@lcwc.ac.uk
www.lcwc.ac.uk

University of Lancashire
Tel: 01772 892444
Email: cenquiries@uclan.ac.uk
www.lancashire.ac.uk

Lancaster University
Tel: 01524 592 028
Email: ugadmissions@lancaster.ac.uk
www.lancaster.ac.uk

University of Leeds
Tel: 0113 3437000
Email: study@leeds.ac.uk
www.leeds.ac.uk

Leeds Beckett University
Tel: 0113 812 3113
Email: admissionenquiries@leedsbeckett.ac.uk
www.leedsbeckett.ac.uk

Leeds City College
Tel: 0113 386 1997
Email: contact@leedscitycollege.ac.uk
www.leedscitycollege.ac.uk

Leeds College of Art
Tel.: 0113 202 8000
Email: admissions@leeds-art.ac.uk
www.leeds-art.ac.uk

Leeds College of Building
Tel: 0113 222 6002
Email: info@lcb.ac.uk
www.lcb.ac.uk

University of Leicester
Tel: 0116 2525281
Email: admissions@le.ac.uk
www.le.ac.uk

Leicester College
Tel: 0116 224 2240
www.leicestercollege.ac.uk

Lewisham Southwark College
Tel: 020 3757 3000
Email: info@lewisham.ac.uk
www.lewisham.ac.uk

Appendix 1: Institution Contact Details

University of Lincoln
Tel: 01522 882000
Email: enquiries@lincoln.ac.uk
www.lincoln.ac.uk

Lincoln College
Tel: 01522 876000
Email: enquiries@lincolncollege.ac.uk
www.lincolncollege.ac.uk

University of Liverpool
Tel: 0151 794 5927
Email: irro@liverpool.ac.uk
www.liv.ac.uk

Liverpool Hope University
Tel: 0151 291 3111
Email: courses@hope.ac.uk
www.hope.ac.uk

The Liverpool Institute for Performing Arts
Tel: 0151 330 3084
Email: admissions@lipa.ac.uk
www.lipa.ac.uk

Liverpool John Moores University (LJMU)
Tel: 0151 231 5090
Email: courses@ljmu.ac.uk
www.ljmu.ac.uk

Coleg Llandrillo
Tel: 01492 542338
Email: generalenquiries@gllm.ac.uk
www.gllm.ac.uk

ARU London (LCA Business School)
Tel: 020 7400 6789
Email: enquiry@london.aru.ac.uk
https://lca.anglia.ac.uk

The London College, UCK
Tel: 020 7243 4000
Email: admissions@lcuck.ac.uk
www.lcuck.ac.uk

London Metropolitan University
Tel: 020 7133 4200
www.londonmet.ac.uk

London South Bank University
Tel: 020 7815 7500
www.lsbu.ac.uk

Loughborough University
Tel: 01509 222222
Email: enquiries@lboro.ac.uk
www.lboro.ac.uk

The University of Manchester
Tel: 0161 306 6000
Email: study@manchester.ac.uk
www.manchester.ac.uk

The Manchester College
Tel: 0333 322 2444
Email: enquiries@tmc.ac.uk
www.tmc.ac.uk

Manchester Metropolitan University
Tel: 0161 247 2000
www.mmu.ac.uk

Coleg Menai
Tel: 01492 542338
Email: generalenquiries@gllm.ac.uk
www.gllm.ac.uk

Middlesex University
Tel: 020 8411 5555
www.mdx.ac.uk

Milton Keynes College
Tel: 01908 684444
Email: info@mkcollege.ac.uk
www.mkcollege.ac.uk

Mont Rose College
Tel: 020 8556 5009
Email: info@mrcollege.ac.uk
www.mrcollege.ac.uk

Morley College London
Tel: 020 7450 1889
www.morleycollege.ac.uk

Newcastle College
Tel: 0191 200 4000
Email: enquiries@ncl-coll.ac.uk
www.newcastlecollege.co.uk

Newcastle University
Tel: 0191 208 6000
www.ncl.ac.uk

New City College
Tel: 0330 135 9000
Email:info@nncclondon.ac.uk
www.ncclondon.ac.uk

New College Durham
Tel: 0191 375 4210
Email: admissions@newdur.ac.uk
www.newcollegedurham.ac.uk

New College Swindon
Tel: 01793 611470
Email: info@newcollege.ac.uk
www.newcollege.ac.uk

North Lindsey College
Tel: 01724 294125
Email: enquiries@ucnl.ac.uk
www.northlindsey.ac.uk

North Warwickshire & South Leicestershire College
Tel: 0330 058 3000
Email: enquiries@nwslc.ac.uk
www.nwslc.ac.uk

University of Northampton
Tel: 0300 303 2772
Email: admissions@northampton.ac.uk
www.northampton.ac.uk

Northeastern University London
Tel: 020 7637 4550
Email: info@nulondon.ac.uk
www.nulondon.ac.uk

Northern School of Art
Tel: 01642 288888
Email: studentrecruitment@northernart.ac.uk
www.northernart.ac.uk

Northumberland College
Tel: 0330 770 6000
Email: info@northland.ac.uk
www.northumberland.ac.uk

Northumbria University
Tel: 0191 406 0901
Email: bc.applicantservices@northumbria.ac.uk
www.northumbria.ac.uk

Norwich University of The Arts
Tel: 01603 610561
Email: studentrecruitment@nua.ac.uk
www.norwichuni.ac.uk

Nottingham College
Tel: 0115 9100 100
Email: enquiries@nottinghamcollege.ac.uk
www.nottinghamcollege.ac.uk

The University of Nottingham
Tel: 0115 951 5151
www.nottingham.ac.uk

Appendix 1: Institution Contact Details

Nottingham Trent University
Tel: 0115 8482999
Email: enquiries@ntu.ac.uk
www.ntu.ac.uk

Oaklands College
Tel: 01727 737000
Email: info@oaklands.ac.uk
www.oaklands.ac.uk

University Campus Oldham
Tel: 0161 344 8800
Email: info@uco.oldham.ac.uk
www.uco.oldham.ac.uk

Oxford Brookes University
Tel: 01865 535000
Email: admissions@brookes.ac.uk
www.brookes.ac.uk

Oxford University
Tel: 01865 270000
www.ox.ac.uk/apply

Petroc
Tel: 01271 345291
Email: reception@petroc.ac.uk
www.petroc.ac.uk

Plumpton College
Tel: 01273 890454
www.plumpton.ac.uk

Arts University Plymouth
Tel: 01752 203400Email: admissions@pca.ac.uk
www.aup.ac.uk

University of Plymouth
Tel: 01752 585858
Email: admissions@plymouth.ac.uk
www.plymouth.ac.uk

University of Portsmouth
Tel: 023 9284 5566
Email: admissions@port.ac.uk
www.port.ac.uk

Queen's University Belfast
Tel: 028 9097 3838
Email: admissions@qub.ac.uk
www.qub.ac.uk

Queen Mary University of London
Tel: 020 7882 5555
Email: admissions@qmul.ac.uk
www.qmul.ac.uk

Ravensbourne
Tel: 020 3040 3500
Email: hello@rave.ac.uk
www.ravensbourne.ac.uk

University of Reading
Tel: 0118 378 8372
Email: ugadmissions@reading.ac.uk
www.reading.ac.uk

Regent's University London
Tel: 020 7487 7625
Email: admit@regents.ac.uk
www.regents.ac.uk

Robert Gordon University
Tel: 01224 262000
Email: admissions@rgu.ac.uk
www.rgu.ac.uk

University of Roehampton
Tel: 020 8392 3232
Email: enquiries@roehampton.ac.uk
www.roehampton.ac.uk

Rose Bruford College
Tel: 020 8308 2600
Email: enquiries@bruford.ac.uk
www.bruford.ac.uk

Rotherham College
Tel: 01709 362111
Email: info@rotherham.ac.uk
www.rotherham.ac.uk

Royal Central School of Speech and Drama, University of London
Tel: 020 7722 8183
Email: admissions@cssd.ac.uk
www.cssd.ac.uk

Royal Conservatoire of Scotland
Tel: 0141 332 4101
Email: admissions@rcs.ac.uk
www.rcs.ac.uk

Runshaw College
Tel: 01772 642040
Email: welcometorunshaw@runshaw.ac.uk
www.runshaw.ac.uk

Ruskin College Oxford
Tel: 01865 759600
Email: enquiries@ruskin.ac.uk
www.ruskin.ac.uk

SAE Institute
Tel: 0333 011 2315
Email: ukadmissions@sae.edu
www.sae.edu

The University of Salford
Tel: 0161 295 5000
Email: course-enquiries@salford.ac.uk
www.salford.ac.uk

Selby College
Tel: 01757 211000
Email: info@selby.ac.uk
www.selby.ac.uk

The University of Sheffield
Tel: 0114 222 2000
Email: admissions@sheffield.ac.uk
www.sheffield.ac.uk

Sheffield College
Tel: 0114 260 2600
Email: info@sheffcol.ac.uk
www.sheffcol.ac.uk

Sheffield Hallam University
Tel: 0114 225 5555
Email: enquiries@shu.ac.uk
www.shu.ac.uk

Shrewsbury Colleges Group
Email: info@scg.ac.uk
www.scg.ac.uk

Coleg Sir Gâr/Carmarthenshire College
Tel: 01554 748000
Email: admissions@colegsirgar.ac.uk
www.colegsirgar.ac.uk

Solihull College
Tel: 0121 678 7000
Email: enquiries@solihull.ac.uk
www.solihull.ac.uk

South and City College Birmingham
Tel: 0121 694 5000
Email: admissions@sccb.ac.uk
www.sccb.ac.uk

University of Southampton
Tel: 023 8059 5000
Email: enquiries@southampton.ac.uk
www.southampton.ac.uk

Appendix 1: Institution Contact Details

Southampton Solent University
Tel: 023 8201 5066
Email: admissions@solent.ac.uk
www.solent.ac.uk

South Devon College
Tel: 0800 0380 123
Email: enquiries@southdevon.ac.uk
www.southdevon.ac.uk

South Essex College
Tel: 0345 521 2345
Email: learning@southessex.ac.uk
www.southessex.ac.uk

South Gloucestershire and Stroud College
Tel: 0800 0567 253
Email: info@sgscol.ac.uk
www.sgscol.ac.uk

South Thames College
Tel: 020 8918 7777
Email: info@south-thames.ac.uk
www.south-thames.ac.uk

South Tyneside College
Tel: 0191 427 3500
Email: student.services@stc.ac.uk
www.stc.ac.uk

Southport College
Tel: 01704 392704
Email: guidance@southport.ac.uk
www.southport.ac.uk

University of South Wales
Tel: 03455 767778
www.southwales.ac.uk

Spurgeon's College
Tel: 020 8683 0850
Email: enquiries@spurgeons.ac.uk
www.spurgeons.ac.uk

Staffordshire University
Tel: 01782 294000
www.staffs.ac.uk

Stamford College
Tel: 01780 484300
Email: enquiries@stamford.ac.uk
www.stamford.ac.uk

Stockport College
Tel: 0161 296 5000
Email: heenquiries@tcg.ac.uk
www.stockport.ac.uk

University Centre St Helens
Tel: 01744 733766
Email: enquire@sthelens.ac.uk
www.sthelens.ac.uk

The University of Strathclyde
Tel: 0141 552 4400
Email: ug.admissions@strath.ac.uk
www.strath.ac.uk

University of Suffolk
Tel: 01473 338833
www.uos.ac.uk

Sunderland College
Tel: 0300 770 8000
Email: info@sunderlandcollege.ac.uk
www.sunderlandcollege.ac.uk

University of Sunderland
Tel: 0191 515 2000
Email: student.helpline@sunderland.ac.uk
www.sunderland.ac.uk

University of Surrey
Tel: 01483 682222
www.surrey.ac.uk

Teesside University
Tel: 01642 218121
Email:enquiries@tees.ac.uk
www.tees.ac.uk

Truro and Penwith College
Tel: 01872 305000
Email: enquiry@truro--penwith.ac.uk
www.truro-penwith.ac.uk

Tyne Metropolitan College
Tel: 0191 229 5000
Email: enquiries@tynemet.ac.uk
www.tynemet.ac.uk

UCL (University College London)
Tel: 020 7679 2000
www.ucl.ac.uk

Ulster University
Tel: 028 9536 5117
Email: r.cullen@ulster.ac.uk
www.ulster.ac.uk

Wakefield College
Tel: 01924 789789
Email: info@wakefield.ac.uk
www.wakefield.ac.uk

University of Wales Trinity St David
Tel: 01267 676767
Email: admissions@uwtsd.ac.uk
www.uwtsd.ac.uk

Walsall College
Tel: 01922 657000
www.walsallcollege.ac.uk

Warrington Collegiate
Tel: 01925 494400
Email: learner.services@warrington.ac.uk
www.warrington.ac.uk

Warrington and Vale Royal College
Tel: 01925 494494
Email: learner.services@wvr.ac.uk
www.wvr.ac.uk

Warwickshire College Group
Tel: 0300 456 0049
Email: info@warwickshire.ac.uk
www.wcg.ac.uk

West London College
Tel: 020 8741 1688
Email: lis@wlc.ac.uk
www.wlc.ac.uk

University of West London
Tel: 0800 036 8888
Email: courses@uwl.ac.uk
www.uwl.ac.uk

University of the West of England, Bristol (UWE)
Tel: 0117 328 3333
Email: admissions@uwe.ac.uk
www.uwe.ac.uk

University of the West of Scotland
Tel: 0800 027 1000
Email: ask@uws.ac.uk
www.uws.ac.uk

University of Westminster
Tel: 020 7915 5000
Email: course-enquiries@westminster.ac.uk
www.westminster.ac.uk

Appendix 1: Institution Contact Details

Weston College
Tel: 01934 411411
www.weston.ac.uk

Weymouth College
Tel: 01305 761100
Email: sue–dafter@weymouth.ac.uk
www.weymouth.ac.uk

Wigan and Leigh College
Tel: 01942 761600
Email: applications@wigan-leigh.ac.uk
www.wigan-leigh.ac.uk

Wirral Metropolitan College
Tel: 0151 551 7777
Email: wmc.enquiries@wmc.ac.uk
www.wmc.ac.uk

University of Wolverhampton
Tel: 01902 323505
Email: admissions@wlv.ac.uk
www.wlv.ac.uk

University of Worcester
Tel: 01905 855111
Email: admissions@worc.ac.uk
www.worcester.ac.uk

Wrexham University
Tel: 01978 293439
Email: enquiries@wrexham.ac.uk
www.wrexham.ac.uk

Writtle College
Tel: 01245 424200
Email: admissions-fe@aru.ac.uk
www.aru.ac.uk/writtle-college

Yeovil College
Tel: 01935 845454
Email: university.centre@yeovil.ac.uk
www.yeovil.ac.uk

University of York
Tel: 01904 324000
Email: ug-admissions@york.ac.uk
www.york.ac.uk

York College
Tel: 01904 770100
Email: info@yorkcollege.ac.uk
www.yorkcollege.ac.uk

York St John University
Tel: 01904 876598
Email: admissions@yorksj.ac.uk
www.yorksj.ac.uk

The colleges and universities in Appendix 1 are listed on the UCAS website as they offer higher education courses (HND courses, degree and Foundation degree courses). Some Foundation providers offer further education courses only and so are not listed. Direct applications for these colleges can be made through their websites. The University of the Arts London comprises six colleges: Central Saint Martins, Chelsea School of Art, London College of Communication, Wimbledon School of Art, Camberwell School of Art and London College of Fashion; courses offered by these colleges are listed under the University of the Arts course details.

Appendix 2: Glossary

Studying art and design

Art Foundation
A one-year further education course offered by universities and colleges, commonly taken by students who want to apply for art or design degree courses at university.

Art school
University departments of art and/or design and stand-alone colleges specialising in the teaching of art and design are commonly referred to as art schools.

Clearing
Students who have applied for degree courses but either have no offers or who have not achieved the required grades for their offers in August can use the UCAS Clearing scheme to apply to other universities.

Extra
Students who have applied for degree courses but who receive no offers can approach more universities from February of the year they intend to go to university using the UCAS Extra system.

Foundation degree
A two-year higher education course.

Further education course
A course below degree level, such as a Foundation course.

Higher education course
A degree-level course.

Higher National Diploma (HND)
A higher education course, often of two years' duration. On some HND courses, students can add a third year to reach degree level.

Portfolio
This can refer either to the case in which an artist carries his or her work or to a body of work that represents the artist's areas of specialisation or interest.

UCAS
The Universities and Colleges Admissions Service, the centralised university applications system for degree course applications.

UCAS Postgraduate
The UCAS system for postgraduate applications to selected universities.

Ways of describing art and design

(NB: these are general descriptions, not definitions, and there are as many ways of categorising types of art and design as there are styles of art itself – and no two people will ever agree on exact definitions.)

Abstract art
Art that relies on colour, shape and form to evoke feelings and emotions; or to express ideas.

Architecture
The design of structures and buildings.

Art
What is art? A good question, and one that people have been asking ever since prehistoric man drew pictures of animals on cave walls. For many people, art is a way of communicating their hopes, fears, beliefs or feelings in a predominantly visual way.

Art history
The study of how changes in styles of painting, sculpture and architecture throughout history relate to or are caused by social, technological or political changes and events.

Ceramics
The design and creation of objects using clay or related materials.

Conceptual art
A work of art in which the idea behind the piece is more important than the actual piece itself.

Contextual studies
The study of the theory of art, taking into account political and social influences, the use of materials and techniques.

Crafts
Work created in studios that has a practical use, such as pottery, jewellery and glassware, typically handmade.

Design
Designers create things or ideas that can be used for practical purposes, for example, websites, furniture and clothing.

Environmental art
Art created out of natural materials as part of the landscape.

Fashion
The design and production of clothes, shoes or accessories, such as handbags.

Figurative art
Art that recognisably depicts people or things.

Fine art
Fine art courses cover the traditional elements of art, such as painting, drawing and sculpture. Fine art practitioners generally focus on producing works that create emotional responses rather than having practical uses.

Performance art
Art that relies on the artist using him- or herself, or other participants, as the artwork.

Photography
The use of light to create still or moving images on light-sensitive surfaces. Photography courses can include film and video.

Printmaking
Creating images by transferring ink or other pigments onto paper, cloth or other surfaces using another surface, such as wood, etched metals, silk screens and so on.

Textiles
Creating cloth using techniques such as felt-making, knitting and weaving.